Why Do We Hurt?

The Problem(s) of Pain

C. Nathan Vannatta

WESTBOW
PRESS*
A DIVISION OF THOMAS NELSON
& ZONDERVAN

WestBow Press books may be ordered through booksellers or by contacting:

WestBow Press
A Division of Thomas Nelson & Zondervan
1663 Liberty Drive
Bloomington, IN 47403
www.westbowpress.com
844-714-3454

ISBN: 978-1-6642-9547-6 (sc)
ISBN: 978-1-6642-9546-9 (hc)
ISBN: 978-1-6642-9548-3 (e)

Library of Congress Control Number: 2023905042

Print information available on the last page.

WestBow Press rev. date: 04/10/2023

For Kelsey and Twila,
who taught me to live out
what I have written down.

Contents

Introduction

Why do we hurt?

This is a question we all face. It is a question that has been asked through all of history. It is a question that confronts all people—asked by the rich and the poor, the slave and the free, the weak and the powerful, the intellectuals and the pragmatics. It is a question I'm sure you have faced. It is a question I have faced. It is a question I encounter regularly in my clinical practice as a physical therapist.

So answering it not only has very real ramifications for how we handle the challenges of each and every day, but it also leads to more abstract sorts of questions. You know, those questions about the fundamental nature of the universe. Why is there so much evil and suffering? How can we stop it? What is the purpose for it? Is there even a purpose? And, for many, if there is a god, why does he, she, or it allow all this to continue? In fact, this issue is one of the common unanswered questions given as a reason for not believing in God.[1] And it is *the* question that we will be taking head-on together in the pages of this book.

---

[1] Austin Cline, "Why don't atheists believe in gods?" Learn Religions, last modified July 13, 2018, https://www.learnreligions.com/why-atheists-dont-believe-in-gods-248065. Pewresearch.org lists "questioning of religious teaching" as the most common reason atheists do not identify with religion ("Why America's 'Nones' don't identify with a religion," Pew Research Center, last modified August 8, 2018, https://www.pewresearch.org/fact-tank/2018/08/08/why-americas-nones-dont-identify-with-a-religion/).

To help understand this question, there is a lot that we can draw from our personal experiences with physical pain. Understanding the physiology of pain provides an illustration for the broader experience of pain we see in the world around us. That is the primary perspective that I hope to offer with this book. However, making that application of our lived experience through physical pain to the broader experience of physical and moral suffering throughout the world, in general, necessitates a discussion of other components of how we each view the world. Because of that, this book will also discuss elements of philosophy and theology and how those are important parts of each of our worldviews.

I personally hold a Christian worldview informed by a biblical theology as best as I can ascertain it. So I will be answering this question from that perspective and also addressing many of the challenges to the Christian faith that I have encountered through this question.

At this point, I bet some of you perusing this introduction—trying to determine if this is a book worth reading—are now thinking, *Good grief! Another Christian self-help book! Probably just another person trying to brand his own approach to Christianity.* Or, *Add it to the list—another high-minded philosopher sitting back in his armchair, sipping brandy, and moralizing the world's pain and suffering.*

I am not going to deny that addressing the question of pain and suffering in the world from an intellectual perspective can often appear convoluted, cold, and without compassion. And I admit that I, too, have read books that seemed to philosophize the reality of pain and suffering into an abstract oblivion that made applying anything that was being said all but impossible. But I will be quick to add that there is a place in the conversation for these more intellectual discussions.

I will also admit that I have read books and articles that are amazingly superficial and that seem to say, "Pain is just a result of your sin. Turn to God, repent, and all will be well." Or, "You of little faith! Just claim your healing! Believe, and God will take this trial from you!" These resources don't seem to take seriously the complexities of individual situations. They don't seem to appreciate the intricacies of unique circumstances. And it feels that they offer only pat answers that leave you feeling invalidated and not helped (despite their claimed intention). Yet there is some truth in these sentiments, and we don't want to fall into the trap of believing that *my situation is the exception to every rule.*

So I don't mean to add *just another book* to the plethora of literature and opinions out there. I want to offer a unique perspective on an age-old question. What perspective is that? Thanks for asking! Let me give you some of my background.

My interest in this topic was spurred while I was an undergraduate student. My wife and I married between my sophomore and junior years of college. During this time, she was going through a particularly challenging season in her life. She had had years of chronic pain, which had led to several appointments with numerous doctors with different training and philosophies. She had received multiple different opinions and recommendations on treatment, but pain persisted, a definitive diagnosis remained elusive, and the limitations on her activity ebbed and flowed with the severity of her pain.

I was studying physics in a pre-engineering track and was planning on attending medical school with a desire to become a team physician in sports medicine. But as her pain continued, I felt increasingly helpless in my ability to do anything for her. I did not understand what was going on (medically or physiologically), which led to me being confused at the vast array of symptoms she would experience. My confusion quickly led to frustration (because I hate not being able to understand things!). And when I am frustrated, it is really hard to be sympathetic, and instead of being patient and kind, I often become short-tempered and abrasive (maybe you can relate).

In response to this, I felt I needed to understand what was causing my wife to suffer from such pain. So I began to read—and read a lot! I read as much as I could find through medical databases and physiology texts about pain and the theories behind it. This pursuit, along with other circumstantial situations, led me to change my course of study. I moved from engineering to a more interdisciplinary program that merged a wider variety of fields. This allowed me to combine a lot of the studying I was doing on pain into the coursework I would need to graduate and also let me continue to study engineering principles in biomechanics (which was a huge interest of mine).

Further, I found what was probably the most helpful thing I was able to do for my wife during this challenging time was not acquiring all of the knowledge and facts about how scientists believe pain works but to be in the day-to-day walk *with* her. Being a consistent presence for her—attempting to understand what was going on in her body and how that was affecting her mind and *heart*. And through that process, I discovered that whatever health care career I ended up in, I wanted to be able to do that with people. I wanted to be able to walk with them through their pain, injury, or illness.

As I was learning more about practice patterns among various health professions, I ended up pursuing a degree in physical therapy, as its practice reflected this idea very closely. It also had a large emphasis on understanding human movement and musculoskeletal injuries—which just happened to be my primary medical interest! And unbeknownst to me at the time, the study of pain neuroscience was a burgeoning field in the physical therapy world. This has allowed me to continue my studies in the complex physiology of pain and advance my understanding of how it works and how to walk with and guide people through it!

So through a little divine providence (at least that's what I believe), I ended up in a different profession than I had planned but still work in a similar field in a manner that I very much enjoy! But what does all of that have to do with this book? Well, I have found that when people experience severe injury or struggle with persistent pain, their questions are not only "How do I get better?" and "What is causing my pain?" (although those are usually questions patients ask). But perhaps one of the more pressing questions people have (and one that people are not always open with) is "Why did this happen to me?" Put another way, "What did I do to deserve this?" Or, for the Christian, "God, why did You let this happen?"

And this is the line of questioning that I want to bring into perspective. When we are in the pressure cooker of life, when our comforts are stripped away, when our plans for the future are threatened, when what comes next is uncertain, doubt has a way of creeping in. Anxiety rises to the surface, and fear grips us. It is in these circumstances that we often begin to ask deeper questions. We start to look beyond concerns of "What if I can't play in the next football game or soccer match?" Or "What if I am not able to walk or run anymore?" Even "What if I can't go back to my job?" To more fundamental questions like, "Why is there so much suffering in this world?" and, "God, I thought You wanted to bless us. I thought You said You were loving and kind. I don't feel loved by this, and this certainly does *not* feel kind! What is going on here?" And for some, the questioning goes so far as to ask, "How can a good and loving God allow something like this? How could He sit back and watch me suffer day in and day out and not stop it?"

These are often the more haunting questions that people face— not "Hey, Doc, can you tell me which nerves are signaling my brain right now and what my functional MRI shows?" Often, the more challenging aspect of our pain experiences is in finding the purpose behind it. *Why* do we hurt?

That is a question that medicine, science, physiology, and neurology cannot answer. That is a philosophical question that will depend on one's underlying worldview and theology. But even those beliefs will interact with one's biology and affect the experience, the recovery, and the outcome (we will get into that in more detail later). But that is why I am writing this book. I want to help us understand that the question of suffering and pain, although complex, is not entirely beyond our understanding. We can find reasons for it. It does not disprove God. And it does not make Christian beliefs contradictory. But it does demand a broad perspective and analysis from multiple viewpoints.

C. S. Lewis recognized this complexity and aptly referred to the reality of evil and its resultant suffering as "The Problem of Pain."[2] Now, not only is the fact of pain a problem in and of itself (because it usually presents as a situation that we want to solve and fix), but it also poses to us several problems in other arenas.

We can outline the problems of pain like this:

1. A pervasive problem
2. The paradigm problem
3. The philosophical problem
4. The physiological problem
5. The personal problem
    a. The personal problem in principle
    b. The personal problem in practice
6. The pastoral problem
    a. Helping in pain
    b. Hoping through pain

So I want to be comprehensive (but not exhausting!) and look at the question through several lenses. I will use a narrative style, inviting you to join me in thinking through this very challenging topic. Also, I adapt stories and experiences from my clinical practice and research to help demonstrate principles and ideas that we will be discussing in more detail with each chapter.[3]

The first chapters will approach the question on a more philosophical level and treat it intellectually. Then we will take a

---

[2] C. S. Lewis, *The Problem of Pain* (New York, NY: HarperOne, 1996). Originally published in 1940.

[3] Although these stories are inspired by actual encounters, several details surrounding the interactions have been fictionalized to protect privacy.

more detailed look at pain neurophysiology in order to understand the amazing complexities of the individual experiences in pain and how that can aid our understanding of pain and suffering at large. Having that background in the underlying questions of pain from philosophical and scientific perspectives, I will turn our attention to what we can discover from God's Word in the Bible—because that is ultimately where we will find the answer to this question!

With that more intellectual consideration of pain (giving us a broad view of the topic and various perspectives on it), we will then address the more personal side and how we can wrestle with the pain and suffering in our own lives and help those around us who are also suffering.

Lastly, I want to preface this by saying that I don't know all the difficulties that anyone reading this has faced or what you are currently going through. So because of that, when we address this question intellectually, you may find some of this abrasive and terse. But bear with me! I don't mean to be insensitive. It is just that there *is* an intellectual side to this question that must be answered concretely. Don't worry; we will also cushion those answers with the more personal side, the pastoral side, the practical side. Also, when I use some understatement, sarcasm, or my incredibly clever wit to introduce some humor, please do not be offended, as my intention is just to lighten the load of this very heavy topic. So know ahead of time that I take this issue very seriously.

Having said that, what I want everyone to know is that pain— the world's pain, people's pain, your pain—it hurts. It is hard. It causes doubts, fears, anxieties, stress, and heartache. Whatever you are facing, I don't want to minimize. I want to validate that this is a hard reality and make clear that my goal with this book is to provide a firm foundation to anchor you, to give you strength, to give you comfort, and to give you hope from which you can experience the "peace that surpasses understanding" (Philippians 4:7).

So here, my Christian beliefs will be made clear. I encourage all who read this book, Christian or not, to consider the idea that

that foundation—that peace—is found in our Lord and Savior, Jesus Christ. For those Christians reading this, we can see this in Hebrews 2:18: "For since He [Jesus Christ] himself was tempted in that which He has suffered, He is able to come to the aide of those who are tempted" (NASB).

Jesus *suffered*, just as we do. And He experienced it to *help* us.

The author of Hebrews goes on to say, "Therefore, since we have a great high priest who has gone through the heavens, Jesus the Son of God, let us hold firmly to the faith we profess. For we do not have a high priest who is unable to sympathize with our weaknesses, but we have one who has been tempted in every way, just as we are— yet was without sin. Let us then approach the throne of grace with confidence, so that we may receive mercy and find grace to help us in our time of need" (4:14–16).

Jesus was acquainted with suffering. He was even tempted by that suffering. He knew it. He felt it. He experienced it on the cross. Yet He conquered it through His resurrection. And not only that, but He is with us in our own suffering. We can approach Him, and He will draw near, never leaving us or forsaking us. Because of this, we are able to "receive *mercy* and find *grace* in our time of need." Jesus knows our suffering. He sympathizes with it and has ultimately overcome it. And in that, I have hope, and I pray that those who read this would have a greater understanding of that hope as well.

With that goal for a foundation of hope established, we can now begin to look at the question and address it. So why do we hurt?

1

A Pervasive Problem

"Do I ask her about it?" came the question from one of the residents during an afternoon mentoring session.

"Well, what do you want to know about it?" I asked, trying to draw out more of his reasoning process.

"I guess I just want to know how she is doing."

"OK, I can see that. That's thoughtful of you. But will it impact your plan of care? Will you adjust your treatment plan because of that?"

"Maybe. I guess that depends on how she answers but probably not."

"I agree. It might be important, but it's not definitively going to impact our treatment. It's certainly good for us to know though, right? So let's stick with our normal interview and gather her history and see what information she offers us. We will want to pay careful attention to how she answers though—what words she uses, how she frames her situation, and what her overall outlook is on her situation. These sorts of things may tip us off to whether there are things that we need to draw out or that we want to ask her about or follow up with her counselor on."

We were briefing on an evaluation he was going to be conducting in a few minutes. We had just finished our chart review on a teenage girl coming to see us for knee pain. And when going through her history, we noted that she had been discharged from the hospital a few months ago after an attempted suicide. This was an obvious clue that there was more going on under the surface than just her knee hurting.

The resident led the subjective interview very similar to how we would complete a normal evaluation: How are you? Have you been to our department before? What brings you in? And so on.

"So when did your knee pain start?" asked the therapist in training.

"A few years ago."

"What happened a few years ago?"

"I'm not sure. I just remember having gone for a long hike, and it just started hurting afterward."

"Do you remember injuring it? Did you trip or twist your knee at all?"

"No. I didn't notice anything like that on the hike."

"OK. Did you go in to have it looked at right away? And did you notice swelling or bruising or anything like that?"

"No. I just kind of dealt with it. I never had it checked out. I don't remember any bruising, but maybe there was swelling." The inflection in her voice was not very convincing.

"What changed that you are coming in to have this looked at now?" the resident asked with keen awareness of an increasingly complicated situation.

"I'm tired of people making fun of me," came the sheepish reply.

"Making fun of you! What do you mean?"

"Well, some days my knee really hurts, and I have to limp. But other days, it's not as bad, and I can walk pretty normally. Sometimes the pain is bad enough that I ask to sit out from track practice, and sometimes I don't. The other students have started to notice this and think I'm faking it. I even have to make sure that I wear pants loose enough that I can hide my knee brace underneath."

"Hm … I see. That is a tough situation. Kids can be ruthless, can't they? Can you tell me more about why you use a knee brace?"

"The pressure just feels really good on my knee."

"OK, well, that's good that you have one thing that makes it feel better! Are there other things that seem to help with the pain?"

"Just staying off of it."

"Does it still hurt right now though? Just sitting here, can you still feel the pain in your knee?"

"Yeah."

"So even though it helps, it doesn't eliminate the pain?"

"No."

"Are there things that really seem to flare it up? Like are there things that you can say, 'If I do that, I am going to feel it later!'"

"I don't know. It just seems to be bad some days and not as bad other days."

This back and forth continued for another few minutes, and then the resident and I stepped away to discuss our findings thus far and plan the physical examination.

"I don't think I was able to get a straight answer or really any information at all," he confessed right away. "I'm not exactly sure what's going on or where to go from here." I could see that he was trying to brace himself for a critical response, as he did not feel very confident in the way the interview went.

"Actually, we got a lot of very useful information! We know that this is a chronic issue. That the pain isn't bad enough for her to seek care, but the treatment she is receiving because of it is. We know that there is no clear mechanical pattern. There are no definitive provoking activities or things that improve her pain other than a knee brace. We know that she has a big psychosocial yellow flag. We know she has no other systemic symptoms. And from our chart review, we know that she has had a completely clear blood panel and all imaging has been normal from when she saw her primary physician. Does the problem sound like it is coming from her knee?"

"That's where she says it's coming from!"

"Well, right. But is the pattern we are seeing consistent with a knee problem? Can you think of any diagnosis right now that sounds like it would explain the pain in her knee?"

"No."

"Right. So let's put it this way. Is the problem *likely* to be in her knee?" I asked to try to lead him down a different line of thinking.

"No?" came the uncertain reply. "I guess it might not be …"

"OK, good. You can see that we can't say that for sure yet. What do we have to do next then?"

"We have to rule out her knee as the problem!" the resident said with increasing enthusiasm as I could see the light bulb beginning to brighten by the gleam in his eye.

"Exactly! If she has even a relatively clean knee exam, we can be more confident that her pain is being driven by something other than the tissues in her knee. Does that make sense?"

"Yes! I think I know what to do now."

We went back to the patient and proceeded with a thorough evaluation of her knee.

Palpation—not definitively tender, but the patient would kind of squirm and was clearly uncomfortable, but she would just say, "It kind of tickles. That's all."

Range of motion—full.

Strength—firm resistance with no definitive provocation of pain.

Gait—normal with no visible limp.

Functional movement—some wobbling in her control of the knee but not too bad and only a shoulder shrug for a response to whether squats, step downs, and lunges were painful or not.

Special tests for the ligaments and internal structures of her knee—negative.

"Well, what do you think?" I asked as we again briefed in order to determine a treatment plan.

"I guess her knee checked out OK. So I'm not really sure."

"Do you feel more confident or less confident in saying that the knee is not the issue?"

"More confident. But if it is not her knee, what is it?"

"The pain. The pain itself is the *problem* ..."

I think we can all readily recognize the tremendous suffering that exists in the world. But it is important to notice that pain and suffering can take multiple forms. It can come through acts of evil among people. It can come through forces of nature in the form of disasters. It can come through the effects of pathogens or malfunctioning physiological processes in illness and disease. It can come through accidents and injuries (like knee pain). And it can come from the result of our own behavior. Different forms arise from different causes, lead to different issues, lead to different problems and questions, which *should* lead to different answers and solutions. But we will get to that later.

For now, I'd like to focus in on a particular type of pain that I am very familiar with in my clinical practice—musculoskeletal pain. This is a tremendous issue in our world today! The presence of physical pain and injury not only leads to disability (in the short term and sometimes long term), but it also creates a burden on the health care system and on the community surrounding the injured individual, stresses the emotions of the sufferer, and can lead to other complications for both physical and mental health. Unfortunately, the frequency with which the burden of pain is occurring is on the rise.

According to a recent Global Burden of Diseases Study,[4] the prevalence of some kind of disease or injury was over 7.3 billion! Considering that the world population at the time was estimated at

---

[4] GBD 2017 Disease and Injury Incidence and Prevalence Collaborators, "Global, regional, and national incidence, prevalence, and years lived with disability for 354 diseases and injuries for 195 countries and territories, 1990–2017: a systematic analysis for the Global Burden of Disease Study 2017." *Lancet 392, no. 10149 (November 2018):* 1789–1858. https://doi.org/10.1016/S0140-6736(18)32279-7.

about 7.5 billion, we can see that disease, injury, and pain come for us all—pretty much literally every year.

But what is perhaps more striking is that when you add up all of the years lived in disability (as a result of those diseases or injuries) across the entire global population, it amounts to 853 million years living in pain or the results thereof. No matter what your stance is on the age of the earth, that is more years than human beings have even been on the planet! And, unfortunately, that number is on the rise. The number of years that people will live with a disability because of disease or injury has risen 7.2 percent from 1990 to 2017.

If we zoom in and focus on the number one cause of disability in the world, there is one condition that stands high above all the rest: low back pain. Hands down, this condition is the top burden in men and women in the majority of countries across the globe and leads to the highest rates and durations of disability. Just about everyone will suffer from some kind of back pain at some point in their life.[5] It affects all cultures and societies, across the entire life span, and both sexes. But what is perhaps more concerning about back pain is its long-term effects. About one-third of people will go on to experience repeated episodes of pain, and over 10 percent will eventually develop chronic low back pain.[6] Now, when this happens, there are many problems that can arise—some of them obvious and others more insidious.

Let's return to our patient story to see some of these more subtle problems.

We had just finished describing our plan to this young lady and explaining to her how we would like to help. She appeared to be

---

[5] Anthony D. Woolf and Bruce Pfleger, "Burden of major musculoskeletal conditions," *Bulletin of the World Health Organization* 81, no. 9 (November 2003): 646–56.

[6] Anthony Delitto, et al., "Clinical Practice Guideline: Low Back Pain," *Journal of Orthopaedic & Sports Physical Therapy* 42, no. 4 (April 2012): A1–A57.

completely on board, but as she was a young teenager, I just wanted to check in with her parents and make sure they agreed with the treatment plan.

"Is your mom or dad still here, so I can make sure they are OK with our plan?" I asked.

"No. My grandma brought me in this morning."

"Can I call one of them?"

"Well, my dad will still be asleep." Note that at this time, it is eight o'clock on a Monday morning.

"Hm. Well, can I call your mom?"

"I don't live with her anymore. She moved away a few years ago," she said in a tone that implied there was more to that situation than she was communicating.

"I see. Well, here—take my card. Tell your dad that if he has any questions at all, he can call me."

I saw this young lady several times over the next few months. She was punctual, respectful, and funny, carried on good conversations, and overall seemed to be improving very nicely. I often forgot that just a few months ago, she was on a hospital bed recovering from an attempted suicide. But over the weeks, as she continued to talk to me and the physical therapy resident working with me, more of her home situation was shared, which filled in some of the spaces for me—one conversation in particular.

"How does this exercise feel today?" I asked at one of her later appointments.

"I really like this one. It always makes my knee seem to feel better. I don't even feel tempted to take my dad's pills anymore!"

"Wait, what? What do you mean by that?" I asked in surprise.

"Well, sometimes I have thought about using some of my dad's pain medication that he has for his back when my knee would hurt really bad."

"*Have* you taken any of them?" I asked, as I felt that I needed to press into this further.

"No," she said in a way that I was confident I believed her, but I still felt there was more to this.

"OK, good. And *don't* take them! But maybe you could ask him to keep them somewhere where they aren't as available to you?" I suggested, hoping to offer some kind of help into what seemed like was a complicated situation.

"I guess I could, but I doubt it would help! My dad has so many issues. His back seems to always be hurting in some way, so he has a bunch of different medications that he leaves all over the place," she said in a tone that betrayed a lot of suppressed frustration. I let her comment linger as I thought (and prayed!) for wisdom on where to go from here. But this young lady hadn't finished, and she offered the needed information to guide where to go next. "Sometimes I feel like I have to take care of my dad more than he takes care of me. It makes me so mad! Why can't he just figure out his issues instead of making them my problem?" came the exasperated release of emotion.

"That is really hard," I said as gently as I could. "I can see that you really care about your dad. There are very few kids your age who would help a parent the way you do. But you're right. It is not fair that you have to do that; that's not the way it is supposed to be."

When your back hurts, it makes just about any activity painful and difficult to do. When you can't be active, often some of the activities you have to do (like your job and work around your home) become increasingly difficult or seemingly impossible to do. When pain limits your ability to do those things, the people you work for have to absorb the lost work or productivity, and your friends, family, and/or coworkers have to pick up the slack. This is maybe *painful* for them too (like we saw happen for our young lady with knee pain)!

Then if you can't do your work for a long time, eventually you will stop getting paid or at least get paid less. This adds stress and wounds your pride (another type of pain). Not only that, but someone (either a family member, or friend, or the government) is going to have to make up for the lost wages in order to keep paying the bills. As this continues and because you want to get better, you will probably go to several appointments and see if someone can help you get better and back on your feet. But back pain is a black hole of diagnostics in health care, and that makes treating it very difficult, so it is quite possible that you may have to see several different specialists to get some relief.

Sometimes, by the time a patient with chronic back pain ends up on my schedule, he has seen many different providers, has had a surgery at one point, has been on multiple pain medications and antidepressants, has tried chiropractic care, injections, and braces, and now, as a last resort, is going to give physical therapy a try. These treatments obviously cost time and more money, which only exacerbates the pain of the situation. Need I go on?

It is this sort of cycle that leads to the huge economic burden on society and health care systems in chronic pain—namely low back pain, in this case. Some estimates of the annual costs related to low back pain are as high as $90 billion with indirect costs (such as lost wages and productivity) and direct costs estimated as high as $28 billion in the United States alone. A similar story is told in the UK, Sweden, Korea, Australia, and others.[7]

Although low back pain is a behemoth of a problem all its own, this sort of problem resulting from pain is not limited to the low back. Other pain conditions that are in the top ten causes of disability include headaches, neck pain, and other forms of musculoskeletal pain. It has been reported that over one hundred million Americans suffer from some form of persistent pain, with at least twenty-five million of those suffering on a daily basis. Persistent

---

[7] Simon Dagenais, et al., "A systematic review of low back pain cost of illness in the United States and internationally," *The Spine Journal* 8, no. 1 (January-Febuary 2008): 8–20, https://doi.org/10.1016/j.spinee.2007.10.005.

pain conditions result in estimates of $560–635 billion every year.[8] This economic burden takes a toll on the individual, their family, their community, and the health care system at large. Our global population is suffering, and it is a problem.

Now what is very ironic is that not only is the pain itself a problem, but a well-intentioned means of treatment for the pain has resulted in a problem all its own—opioids. The use of narcotic pain medication, although effective in the short term, has been termed an epidemic. Between the years 2000 and 2010, the deaths related to prescription opioids exceeded deaths related to cocaine and heroin combined![9] Not only is there a host of risky side effects related to narcotic pain medications, but they also have a nasty tendency for people to develop a tolerance to them or a dependence on them—or both!

When you have a tolerance to a drug, you have to take more and more of the drug in order to get the same effect. And a dependence is when your body has become so accustomed to having the drug in your system it begins to have symptoms of illness when the drug is no longer present. You actually need the drug in order to maintain your new normal.

Over time, this can make overdosing easier (which increases your risk of death), can make you addicted to the medication itself (which stresses your finances, alters your behavior, and affects your relationships—note father and daughter relationship strain described above), and can actually result in your pain becoming worse! This is known as opioid-induced hyperalgesia.[10] Essentially what happens

---

[8] Richard Nahin, "Estimates of pain prevalence and severity in adults: United States," *The Journal of Pain* 16, no. 8 (August 2015): 769–780, https://doi.org/10.1016/j.jpain.2015.05.002.

[9] Stephen W. Patrick, et al., "Implementation of prescription drug monitoring programs associated with reductions in opioid-related death rates," *Health Affairs* 35, no. 7 (July 2016): 1324–1332, https://doi.org/10.1377/hlthaff.2015.1496.

[10] Seong Heon Lee, et al., "Tramadol induced paradoxical hyperalgesias," *Pain Physician* 16, no. 1 (January 2013):41–44.

here is that the nerves in your body become extremely sensitive because the medication has begun to alter their natural function. This causes the nerves in your body to be triggered easier and can actually lead to more pain.[11]

I would argue that a big problem with the use of opioid medications in the treatment of pain is that they indiscriminately shut down our ability to feel pain with no regard for the cause or purpose of the pain—and do it powerfully! Now this is great when you are coming right out of surgery or just need to be able to lie still to have an x-ray taken after a severe injury, but to use this in a *therapeutic* manner is not without risk—to say the least.[12] And that's because pain serves a purpose, and we need to understand what that purpose is in order to deal with it effectively.

Returning to our discussion of physical pain, we can see that it presents a problem for a variety of people, and undiscerning treatments and attempts to address it (even if well intentioned) can result in other problems like death, addictions, worsening symptoms, and economic burden. Yikes! This is a big problem, isn't it? But let's just think about this a little more.

So, if you were in a lot of pain, a lot of the time, you had seen a lot of providers, received a lot of treatment, spent a lot of money on continuing that treatment, and your symptoms worsened (a lot?), how would you feel?

How many of you included *hopeless* or *depressed* in that list of emotions?

That would be a common response. And there are established links between the use of opioids and depression,[13] depression and

---

[11] Marion Lee, et al., "A comprehensive review of opioid-induced hyperalgesia," *Pain Physician* 14, no. 2 (March-April 2011): 145–161.

[12] Anna Lembke, et al., "Weighing the risks and benefits of chronic opioid therapy," *American Family Physician* 93, no. 12 (June 2016): 982–990.

[13] Jeffrey F. Sherrer, et al., "Prescription opioid duration, dose, and increased risk of depression in 3 large patient populations," *Annals of Family Medicine* 14, no. 1 (January-February 2016): 54–62. https://doi.org/10.1370/afm.1885.

persistent pain,[14] and, unfortunately, in those with persistent pain *and* depression a link with suicide.[15] And this is a very sobering reality.

In that same Global Burden of Disease study we were talking about a little bit ago, there was another condition that squirmed its way into the top ten—a condition that is testament to another form of pain—emotional pain. Depressive disorders are the third leading cause of disability among females and the fifth leading cause of disability in males. There is a very real link between the pain inside of us, the pain we see around us, and how we are able to function in the world. When we ourselves hurt, or we see those we love around us hurting, and continued attempts to relieve or stop that pain are ineffective, it is easy to lose hope, give in, and give up. It affects more than our bodies, minds, and emotions. But it affects our souls (see Proverbs 13:12).

The problem of pain, if it persists and is not handled appropriately, can turn people down a tragic road. The National Vital Statistics report on the leading causes of death in the United States rates self-harm (suicide) as number ten overall, comprising 1.7 percent of all deaths in the United States during 2018.[16] However, if you break down the causes by age, there is a strikingly high rate in young people. Suicide is the second leading cause of death in those aged ten to thirty-four.[17] In 2018, suicide accounted for 10.9 percent and

---

[14] Tamar Pincus, et al., "A systematic review of psychological factors as predictors of chronicity/disability in prospective cohorts of low back pain," *Spine (Phila Pa 1976)* 27, no. 5 (March 2002): E109-20, https://doi.org/10.1097/00007632-200203010-00017.

[15] Mélanie Racine, "Chronic pain and suicide risk: A comprehensive review," *Progress in Neuro-Psychopharmacology & Biological Psychiatry* 87, Pt. B (December 2018): 269–280, https://doi.org/10.1016/j.pnpbp.2017.08.020.

[16] Sherry L. Murphy, et al., "Deaths: Final Data for 2018," *National Vital Statistics Reports*.69, no. 12 (January 2021): 1-83.

[17] "Suicide," Mental Health Infromation: Statistics, National Institute of Mental Health, accessed February 6, 2021, https://www.nimh.nih.gov/health/statistics/suicide.shtml.

20.6 percent of all deaths in those aged ten to fourteen and fifteen to twenty-four years, respectively.[18] Read that again. This fact is heartbreaking. The experience of pain is a problem, the difficulty we have in appropriately dealing with it is a problem, and the impact it is having on the families of those in pain is a problem.

One of the resultant consequences of pain and suffering persisting in adults is that it has the potential to trickle down the generational line and negatively impact the children of those suffering. This is part of the problem that we saw arise in the life of our young lady with knee pain, and this is not happening in isolation.

There is an increasing recognition in the medical field of what have been called adverse childhood experiences (ACEs). An ACE is a stressful or traumatic event that is witnessed or experienced by someone under the age of seventeen. This would include things like abuse, witnessing domestic violence, or the death of a parent and even includes growing up in a household where there is substance abuse (think opioids from earlier), mental health issues (think anxiety and depression), marital strife in the form of divorce or separation, or imprisonment of a household member. It is estimated that 61 percent of adults have experienced at least one ACE during their youth.[19]

On top of this, there is a strong link between children with a history of an adverse experience and the risk of depression.[20] And ACEs have a wide range of effects leading to long-term changes in the nervous, endocrine, and immune systems of children, which

---

[18] These percentages were calculated from the total number of deaths in these age groups from the National Vital and Statistics Report and the total deaths by suicide reported from National Institute of Mental Health.

[19] "Fast Facts: Preventing child abuse and neglect," Injury Center: Violence Prevention, Centers of Disease Control, accessed April 15, 2020, https://www.cdc.gov/violenceprevention/childabuseandneglect/fastfact.html.

[20] Daniel P. Chapman, et al., "Adverse childhood experiences and the risk of depressive disorders in adulthood," *Journal of Affective Disorders* 82, no. 2 (October 2004): 217–225, https://doi.org/10.1016/j.jad.2003.12.013.

can put them at risk for chronic health conditions later in life.[21] This is part of what we saw playing out in the life of that teenager seeing me in the clinic. These sorts of trends suggest that there is a generational effect occurring around these more difficult situations in that the challenges and pain that adults face can impact their children (particularly if not handled appropriately). These can then perpetuate future problems for those children, which sets the stage for the cycle to continue. On and on it goes ...

As a nation, we are seeing the devastating impact of this problem on our young people. Teen anxiety and depression is on the rise, prompting *Time* magazine to devote a special issue to this problem in its first periodical of November 2016. And who can blame them? When young people are facing unstable homes, witnessing struggles with chronic pain, substance use (or abuse), and sometimes violence at high rates, this is certainly a dire situation, and its effect is *pervasive*. It is a problem that affects all people.

I am going to forgo talking about the effects and devastation caused by natural disasters, wars, or the inhumane crimes that people commit against one another. You can just grab a newspaper, check your news feed, or turn on the evening news broadcast to get the evidence you need to demonstrate that those things happen all the time and affect each of us in various ways. So the problem of pain and suffering is one that we all experience in one way or another.

Have I made my point? Can we agree that the existence of suffering and pain is virtually undeniable? And physical pain is a particularly prevalent problem that has far-reaching effects for the individual and those around them. The effects of pain in our world are felt and witnessed by each of us. And we see tremendous efforts around the world by individuals and organizations to prevent these

---

[21] Andrea Danese and Bruce S. McEwen, "Adverse childhood experiences, allostasis, allostatic load, and age-related disease," *Physiology & Behavior* 106, no. 1 (April 2012): 29–39, https://doi.org/10.1016/j.physbeh.2011.08.019.

things from happening and to assist those in need, yet the problem continues and is becoming worse.

Why has a solution to the various forms of pain and suffering we see in the world been so elusive? Why can't our organizations, governments, and programs fix the problem and stop the pain and suffering? Remember how I said that the indiscriminate use of opioid medications was a problem because it doesn't sort out the underlying cause of pain? Well, I would argue that politics and programs run into the same problem. If policies don't address the underlying cause of pain, their solutions, treatments, and answers won't solve the problem—and could potentially make things worse.

And the problem isn't lack of programs. It isn't a lack of justice or appropriate rehabilitation. It isn't that parents don't know how to raise children. The problem isn't lack of education or the misappropriation of financial resources. The problem isn't oppression of the weak by the strong. Those are all symptoms of the problem. That's not to say that efforts to address those things are bad or useless, but they aren't fixes or cures in and of themselves.

The problem of pain and suffering in our world is more pervasive than that; it is rooted in a deeper, more searching, and very challenging metaphysical problem. I would contend that we won't be able to adequately address the problem of pain until we understand the purpose and the source of pain. And this is a question of how we fundamentally view the world—its origin, its purpose, and its nature. This is inherently a problem of paradigm.

2

The Paradigm Problem

"What do you think? Would going to a chiropractor help for this?" the patient asked me as we were wrapping up his examination of what had now been several months of neck pain.

"It certainly could," I responded. "In theory, a lot of the treatments a chiropractor would do should complement anything that we would do in physical therapy. In fact, we utilize a lot of the same tools like ultrasound and electrical stimulation. And many chiropractic adjustments are very similar to some techniques that physical therapists do. So you could see a chiropractor if you wanted. I would have no problem with that."

"OK, but I don't *have* to see a chiropractor for this to get better?"

"No, I don't think so. I am not aware of any evidence that would say that chiropractic treatment is *necessary* for you to see improvement in your pain. Why do you ask that?" I queried, as I was very intrigued by this question, because the way it was asked seemed to indicate there was more under the surface.

"Well, a friend of mine swears by the chiropractor she goes to and tells me if I would just see this chiropractor, my neck would get better. But I don't know. I just remember hearing my dad say that chiropractors were nothing but quacks! I am just skeptical."

"Ha!" I had to laugh, as I very much appreciated his honesty and frankness. "You know, many chiropractors get a bad rap because of its early theories. At its outset, chiropractors claimed that the majority of bodily ailments were caused by subluxations of the spine and that through identifying where those malalignments were, one could perform an adjustment to restore spinal alignment and cure a whole variety of conditions—even things like the common cold. Now, I too am skeptical of anyone who says that things like the common cold are caused by malalignments of the spine. That doesn't seem to line up with our current understanding of pathology and disease. But many chiropractors no longer hold to that type of underlying theory. And chiropractic treatment that strives to be more in line with what we call evidence-based practice is trying to use a more scientifically established theory for its practice. These efforts are leading to many chiropractors becoming more accepted in the medical community."[22]

"But you think I can get better without going to a chiropractor though?" he asked in a way as if he wanted to gently turn down his friend's advice.

"I think we have a lot of things that I can help you with that will likely lead to improvement in your pain even if you just see me," I responded as diplomatically as I could. "And if your pain is still not improving after a few weeks, or you change your mind and would like to see a chiropractor, there are a few that work in this clinic that I could direct you to—if you would like."

---

[22] The Wikipedia page "Chiropractic" provides a thorough summary of the history of chiropractic theory and practice. It references several peer-reviewed papers, including multiple meta-analyses, systematic reviews, and Cochrane reviews. It also provides a summary of the effectiveness of chiropractic treatment on several commonly treated conditions. This can be accessed at https://en.wikipedia.org/wiki/Chiropractic#Effectiveness. Viewed on February 9, 2021.

"Yeah, OK. That sounds like a good plan," he replied with genuine gratitude.

Now I maybe have just walked myself into a lot of trouble because there is sometimes a perceived tension between physical therapists and chiropractors; a kind of legal turf battle over who can do what sort of treatments has been ongoing for some time. In light of that, I want to be absolutely clear that I am in no way trying to diminish the practice of chiropractors. I am only sharing this story to reference the early theories espoused by the chiropractic profession and how those underlying theories have a large impact on what is eventually done as a mode of treatment. In other words, the original chiropractic paradigm—how it viewed disease and pathology—ultimately determined the avenue of treatment pursued. This is simply an illustration for the point of this chapter.

Let's dig into this a little bit. So chiropractic care was founded by D.D. Palmer in 1895 when he allegedly cured a man's deafness by manipulating his spine. Palmer was a "magnetic healer" who also used techniques from the folk-medicine practice of "bonesetting." He endorsed several mystical views, such as the presence of an "innate intelligence," which was believed to be representative of a "universal intelligence" or "vital force" within each person. There is an obvious theological undertone here, so much so that D.D. Palmer apparently considered establishing chiropractic as a religion.[23]

That being said, the foundational view of illness proposed by Palmer was that the "innate intelligence" regulated all body functions, but "vertebral subluxations" interfered with its appropriate functioning. Hence, correction of "vertebral subluxations" would

---

[23] This paragraph is a summary from a review article published in the *Journal of Pain and Symptom Management*. Edzard Ernst, "Chiropractic: A Critical Evaluation," *Journal of Pain and Symptom Management* 35, no. 5 (May 2008): 544–562, https://doi.org/10.1016/j.jpainsymman.2007.07.004.

restore natural function and cure *all* disease. Yes, *all* disease. According to Palmer's original view, spinal manipulation was a cure for all human illness, stating that "95% of all diseases are caused by displaced vertebrae, the remainder by luxations of other joints."[24]

So, if you believe that all disease stems from a subluxation of a joint, what are you going to do to cure disease? Fix the subluxation, right? Because of this, chiropractic treatment in its original form always consisted of some form of *adjustment*.

Can we see what I am getting at? What we understand as the cause of the problem—or the *paradigm* through which we see and interpret it—ultimately influences (if not determines!) what we attempt to do about it.

Now in wrapping up this illustration, I want to make it clear that many chiropractors today do not embrace the original ideas of D.D. Palmer. And there are efforts to make current chiropractic practice founded on more scientific principles. In fact, there is a lot of literature on the effectiveness of different forms of spinal manipulation—even in the profession of physical therapy.[25] There seems to be some benefit to this mode of treatment, but why and how it works and under what circumstances it is to be applied are areas of ongoing investigation.[26]

So what does this have to do with answering the question of the pain that we see in the world? Well, as we saw in the last chapter, pain is a pervasive problem that affects all people. And we all have a paradigm—a viewpoint or underlying belief system—through which we answer that question. And there are a lot of viewpoints out there!

---

[24] Samuel Homola, *Bonesetting, chiropractic, and cultism* (Panama City, FL: Critique Books, 1963) cited in Ernst, "Chiropractic: A Critical Evaluation," 546.

[25] A simple PubMed search for "spinal manipulation" resulted in 4,882 articles on February 10, 2021.

[26] Joel E. Bialsoky, et al., "Unraveling the Mechanisms of Manual Therapy: Modelling an Approach," *Journal of Orthopedic and Sports Physical Therapy* 48, no. 1 (January 2018): 8–18, https://doi.org/10.2519/jospt.2018.7476.

What are those then? Great question. That's what we are going to get into next. The viewpoints are probably innumerable because, to some degree, people view things uniquely and individually. Nonetheless, how one answers the question "Why do we hurt?" will be influenced by his or her underlying belief system. So, as we search for an answer to this question, we are confronted with the many viewpoints of the world that will influence our answer. Off the top of my head, here are some of the viewpoints that are available out there:

1. Atheism
2. Agnosticism
3. Buddhism
4. Christianity
5. Dualism
6. Hinduism
7. Islam
8. Judaism
9. Panentheism
10. Pantheism
11. Pluralism

This is not an exhaustive list, but to make one would be exhausting! Anyway, there are a lot of different paradigms through which people can answer the question "Why do we hurt?" My goal for the rest of this chapter is to give a *brief* summary of each of these views so that we can see that these are not compatible with one another. Therefore, to embrace one means to exclude the others.[27] This is the nature of truth. To say that something is "this way" is to simultaneously say "it is *not* that way." When a person makes a truth

---

[27] Even if they answer the question of why there is pain in the world in a similar manner, like we will see with the monotheistic religions, they will ultimately differ in how they view Jesus.

claim, or tries to answer a question like the one we are addressing, in a way that is correct, he or she is also saying, or explaining how, other views or explanations are incorrect.

Atheism disagrees with Christianity, Judaism, and Islam in their answer to this question because these views do not agree on the role of a god in the world. Atheism says there is no god to be considered when addressing this question, while Christianity, Judaism, and Islam say there is a god who *must* be considered. These views cannot all be correct because they contradict one another at one point or another. So the problem we run into is which one is correct? Or, at the very least, which view are we going to use to try to answer the question and seek a solution?

In moving forward, I am going to do my best to present an honest and fair summary of each viewpoint. I am not going to evaluate them. Only present them. You can evaluate them yourself. Also, in providing a brief summary, there is no way that I can address all of the different nuances within each of these overarching worldviews. So let it be known that there will be variations within each of these.

Moving in alphabetical order—here we go!

Atheism

For starters, atheism has become a loose term, with many different forms of this worldview being described.[28] So I want to be clear in describing the view that I am presenting. Atheism, in the sense that I am referring to here, is in its strictest definition—that is, to *declare*

---

[28] For example, Norman Geisler lists metaphysical atheism, semantical atheism, conceptual atheism, and practical atheism as different forms that this central ideology can take. See Norman L. Geisler, "Atheism," *The Big Book of Christian Apologetics: An A to Z Guide* (Grand Rapids, MI: Baker Books, 2012), 40.

that no god exists. For those who are uncertain if a god exists, that belief will be discussed with agnosticism.

Because there is such a variety in views regarding how atheism plays out, and there is no central atheistic organization to formalize the tenets of this worldview,[29] I am not aware of a response to "why there is pain and suffering in the world" that would likely be agreed upon by all pronounced atheists. Thus, to represent this view, I think it is most helpful to look at the central tenets of what *atheism* declares and formulate the logical conclusion of those tenets, not to try and refute what this or that *atheist* says. Put another way, I am going to present what belief in *atheism* asserts and only quote what an *atheist* has said as an illustration or example of that assertion.

So *atheism* declares there is no god. As a result, the universe must be eternal because there was nothing else to cause its existence. Carl Sagan writes, "The universe is all there is, all there was, and all there ever will be."[30] Now there is all sorts of debate as to whether the universe we observe today is the permeation of one fluctuating universe or a more complex multiverse, but the consensus seems to be that our presence in the world we observe is either a product of an infinite mind or that of chance—it just is this way.[31] As atheism, by definition, denies God's existence, we are left with chance as the explanation. So, according to atheism, the life we all experience in the world is due to the admission that we just ended up here and this is just the way it is (i.e., chance).

Now if the origin of our existence is chance, there is no purpose behind it and therefore no purpose for it.[32] And if there is no purpose

---

[29] Julian Baggini, *Atheism: A Very Short Introduction*, (New York: Oxford University Press, Inc., 2003). Cited from *Atheism* at https://en.wikipedia.org/wiki/Atheism. Accessed on February 11, 2021.

[30] Carl Sagan, *Cosmos* (New York: Random House, 1980), 4.

[31] Stephen Hawking, *The Illustrated a Brief History of Time: Updated and expanded edition*, (New York: Bantam Dell, 1996), 181.

[32] A belief in purposelessness is actually listed as a presupposition of atheism according to Geisler's *The Big Book of Christian of Christian Apologetics: An*

for life, there is no reason to explain why suffering exists—it just does. As best I can tell, this is the necessary conclusion from atheism, which is clearly shown in this statement from atheist Richard Dawkins:

> In a universe of blind physical forces and genetic replication some people are going to get hurt, other people are going to get lucky, and you won't find any rhyme or reason in it, nor any justice. The universe we observe has precisely the properties we should expect if there is, at the bottom, no design, no purpose, no evil and no other good. Nothing but blind pitiless indifference. DNA neither knows nor cares. DNA just is. And we dance to its music.[33]

In summary, atheism denies god, accepts that existence is due to chance, admits to there being no underlying purpose, and succumbs to the conclusion that pain and suffering just are—it is simply the luck of the draw.

Agnosticism

Agnosticism is a term coined by T. H. Huxley.[34] The word literally means "no knowledge." It stems from the Greek words *a* (which means "no") and *gnosis* (which means "knowledge"). To be agnostic then means to declare "not to know." Now the *knowledge* referred to

---

A to Z Guide, 41.

[33] Richard Dawkins, *Out of Eden,* (New York: Basic Books, 1992), 133. Cited from Ravi Zacharias and Vince Vitale, *Why Suffering? Finding Meaning and Comfort When Life Doesn't Make Sense,* (New York, NY: Faith Words, 2014), 144.

[34] Thomas H. Huxley, "Agnosticism and Christianity." In *Collected Essays,* ed. Frederick Barry (New York: Macmillan, 1929). Cited in Geisler, *The Big Book of Christian Apologetics: An A to Z Guide,* 13.

here is usually in reference to the knowability of God or the ultimate nature of reality, not necessarily to questions like "Why do we hurt?" But by default, to claim "not to know" about the nature of reality leaves you without a framework to answer other questions regarding purpose. Thus, agnosticism honestly declares "not to know" the answer to these sorts of questions regarding purpose.

Buddhism

In stark contrast to agnosticism, Buddhism boldly declares both the reason for pain and suffering and the solution to it. Interestingly, Buddhism was actually founded through the quest of Siddhartha Gautama (later to be known as "the Buddha") to find the path away from "irremediable suffering."[35] The result of his quest was the proclamation of the "Four Noble Truths":[36]

1. The Noble Truth of the *Dukkha* (suffering, dissatisfaction, stress): Life is fundamentally fraught with suffering and disappointment of every description.
2. The Noble Truth of the Cause of *Dukkha*: The cause of this dissatisfaction is *tanha* ([ignorant][37] craving) in all its forms.

---

[35] Roger Eastman, *The Ways of Religion: An Introduction to the Major Traditions*, 3rd edition, (New York: Oxford University Press, 1999), 77.

[36] The following list is cited from L.T. Jeyachandran, "Challenges from Eastern Religions," In *Beyond Opinion*, ed. Ravi Zacharias (Nashville, TN: Thomas Nelson, 2007), 89. This author cites Elizabeth J. Harris, *What Buddhists Believe* (Oxford, UK: Oneworld Publications, 1998), 42–44 as the source for this description of the "Four Noble Truths."

[37] Heinrich Zimmer describes this as an "ignorant craving." That is to be in a state of "non-knowing" about the reality of the world, and our thoughts and feelings are a result of our own conventions about reality. These conventions then lead to the conclusion that the ills of an individual are a "pathological blend of unfulfilled cravings, vexing longings, fears, regrets, and pains." This is a summary from the section titled "Buddhahood" by Heinrich Zimmer in

3. The Noble Truth of the Cessation of *Dukkha*: An end to dissatisfaction can be found through the relinquishment and abandonment of craving.
4. The Noble Truth of the Path Leading to Cessation of *Dukkha*: The method of achieving the end of all suffering is found in the Eightfold Path.

So Buddhism outright declares that the cause of pain is craving (or desire) born out of ignorance to reality, and the solution is to understand the true nature of reality and stop craving (stop desiring) anything. The rest of the religion is a system of practices to achieve the abandonment of craving and/or desire.

Christianity

Christianity believes that the reason that pain and suffering exist is because the world is fallen and under the curse of sin (the disobedience of people against God's commands). The world we find ourselves in is not as it was intended or created to be, but rather we are in a period of waiting for God to redeem His creation (to bring it back to a state of perfection). The suffering that we see in this world is a result of the sin of human beings but is allowed for what could be various reasons. Some of these reasons are to bring people to repentance, to bring judgement on evil, to test the faith of believers, to shape an individual's character, to bring one closer into fellowship with God and/or other believers, or to reveal the person of Jesus Christ, but to ultimately bring about God's purposes.

Christians also believe that God did not turn His back on His creation or abandon them to suffer without Him. Rather, He actually entered into the fallen world as the person of Jesus Christ to suffer with human beings and pay the penalty of sin (through His

Roger Eastman's *The Ways of Religion: An Introduction to the Major Traditions*, 3rd edition (New York, NY: Oxford University Press, 1999), 84.

death on the cross) and to bring people back into a right relationship with Him. He then proved the power of that redemption through His literal and bodily resurrection from the dead three days later.

This is a very brief summary of my understanding of the Christian response to this question, but the next four chapters will be spent developing and defending this position.[38]

Dualism

Dualism (in a metaphysical[39] sense) is the belief that there are two coeternal principles that interact with each other.[40] This would be that there is an eternal back and forth between the fundamental concepts of good and evil. In dualism, good and evil are distinct from each other[41] but are dependent on each other. However, neither is supreme over the other. Rather, good is limited by evil, and evil limited by good. The Western expression of this belief can be seen

---

[38] Forgive the lack of references and citations here. As this is meant to be a summary of a more developed argument in subsequent chapters, I decided to refrain from cluttering the text with references to biblical passages and the works of Christian scholars. For the detailed references and substantiation of these claims, please read on!

[39] This is not to be confused with dualism in an anthropological sense, which states that there are two components to our personhood: a physical component and a spiritual component. There are various understandings of anthropological dualism in philosophy of mind, which is distinct from the metaphysical dualism that is being discussed here. For a discussion of anthropological dualism, I would refer the interested reader to the writings of J. P. Moreland (e.g., "Christianity, Neuroscience, and Dualism" in *The Blackwell Companion to Science and Christianity*, J.B. Stump and Alan G. Padgett, eds. (Malden, MA: Wiley-Blackwell, 2012)).

[40] See summary in Geisler, *The Big Book of Christian Apologetics: An A to Z Guide,* 127.

[41] The Western expression of this is different from the idea of a "dark side" and "light side" of one force like that popularized in *Star Wars*. A universal force with various expressions (i.e., light and dark) is more akin with Taoism.

in Gnosticism and Zoroastrianism, where they see these forces in conflict with each other.[42] An Eastern expression of this idea would be the yin and yang of Taoism. However, the distinction here would be that the idea of yin and yang are balanced principles expressing an underlying cosmic force (Qi) that are in harmony with each other as opposed to in conflict with each other.[43]

Although I think appreciating the distinction between the Western and Eastern expressions of this underlying idea is important, the way this belief in opposite forces answers the question of pain and suffering is ultimately the same. The experience of pain and suffering in the world is the result of the expression of the eternal principle of evil, as opposed to good.

Hinduism

Hinduism is essentially a specific form of polytheism, as its own tradition claims 333,000,000 deities.[44] But it espouses a fundamentally pantheist philosophy[45] in the way it describes the origin of reality as being an expression of a universal, cosmic "existence"—a force or being—that all of existence arose out of and is fundamentally a part of. Consider this statement from the *Chandogya Upanishad*:[46]

---

[42] John D. Kronen and Sandra Messen, "The defensibility of Zoroastrian dualism," *Religious Studies*, 46, no. 2 (June 2010): 185-205, https://doi.org/10.1017/S0034412509990357.

[43] "Religions: Concepts within Taoism," BBC, accessed February 14, 2021, https://www.bbc.co.uk/religion/religions/taoism/beliefs/concepts.shtml.

[44] Mary Pat Fisher, *Living Religions: A Brief Introduction* (Upper Saddle River, NJ: Prentice Hall, 2002), 46.

[45] See L. T. Jeyachandran distinction between "popular Hinduism" and "philosophical Hinduism" and how these different theological views can be embraced in various forms of Hinduism in *Beyond Opinion*, Ravi Zacharias, ed. (Nashville, TN: Thomas Nelson, 2007), 82.

[46] *The Upanishads*. Translated by Swami Prabhavananda and Frederick Manchester. The Vedanta Society of Southern California (New York: Mentor

> In the beginning there was Existence alone—One only, without a second. He, the One, thought to himself: Let me be many, let me grow forth. Thus out of himself he projected the universe, and having projected out of himself the universe, he entered into every being. All that is has its self in him alone. Of all things he is the subtle essence.

When you first read this, you are probably asking, "How can a religion be both polytheistic and pantheistic?" This is a very fair question. It has been suggested that Hinduism is perhaps better understood as a "family of religions" because of its propensity to grow, change, and absorb teachings of other religions.[47] Sarvepalli Radhakrushnan describes "Hinduism [as] a movement, not a position; a process, not a result; a growing tradition, not a fixed revelation."[48] Therefore, the religion is in a constant state of flux and is difficult to characterize. However, given Hinduism's long history and its common profession in one of the world's most populous nations, it warrants being presented independently from these other broader theological categories.

Hinduism is distinguished from other forms of polytheism (or pantheism?) by a group of teachings called the *Vedas*. Therefore, Hinduism can be defined as the religion of "those who honor the teachings of the *Vedas*."[49] So it is to these teachings that we must turn to find how Hinduism answers the question of pain and suffering. In doing this, there is one teaching in particular that is necessary to understand the Hindu response to pain and suffering: *karma*.

Karma at its basic definition means "the sum of a person's actions in this and previous states of existence, viewed as deciding

---

Books, 1957), 46. Cited in Fisher, *Living Religions: A Brief Introduction,* 52.
[47] Eastman, *The Ways of Religion: An Introduction to the Major Religions*, 13.
[48] *The Hindu View of Life*. Macmillan: New York, 1927. Pg. 91 cited in Eastman, *The Ways of Religion: An Introduction to the Major Religions*, 13.
[49] Fisher, *Living Religions: A Brief Introduction*, 46.

their fate in future existences."[50] Hinduism embraces a view that we are all trapped in an eternal cycle of birth, death, and rebirth (called *samsara*) where the weight of good and bad deeds is visited upon each individual in a subsequent rebirth.

Let me quote Mary Pat Fisher from her book on world religions to show the ultimate conclusion from this view:

> Our life is what we have made it. And we ourselves are shaped by what we have done. Not only do we reap in this life the good or evil we have sown; they also follow us after physical death, affecting our next incarnation.[51]

So the answer to the question "Why do we hurt?" according to the Hindu notion of *karma* is that we are each getting what we deserve from something in this life or a previous one.

Islam

Islam is one of the world's three monotheistic religions—Christianity, Judaism, and Islam. Because of the belief in one all-powerful god, these traditions have some degree of overlap in how they view the suffering we see in the world around us. Ultimately, each of these religions frames the reality of suffering within the purposes of god. This is reflected in the Islamic belief that there is one god (Allah) who ultimately has power over all that happens in this world (technically this is referred to as being omnipotent). I think it is interesting to note that in Islam, suffering poses a challenge to Allah's omnipotence, whereas in Christianity and Judaism, suffering

---

[50] Defined by Oxford Languages from a simple Google search of "karma definition."

[51] Fisher, *Living Religions: A Brief Introduction*, 53.

poses a challenge to God's goodness and love.[52] Nonetheless, because the reality of suffering must be interpreted within the understanding of Allah's omnipotence, Muslims (those who are adherents to the Islamic system) believe that suffering must be the "will of Allah" to the extent that any suffering must be coming from him[53]—otherwise it would not be happening. This is stated concisely in the Qur'an:

> No calamity befalls anyone except by Allah's Will.
> (Surah 64:11)[54]

Therefore, if a Muslim is allowed to suffer, it is for one of two reasons: it is either a result of one's sin, or it is a test of faith.[55] We can turn to two passages in the Qur'an that explicitly support these explanations for the suffering experienced by an individual. Surah 4:79 says,

> Whatever good befalls you is from Allah and whatever evil befalls you is from yourselves.[56]

The idea is that if something evil is happening to you, you must have done something to deserve it; otherwise Allah would not have allowed it to "befall you."

However, the Qur'an does recognize that there can be instances of suffering that are not the direct result of a person's own wrongdoing or sin. The other option then is that suffering is meant to prove one's faith as a trial. Surah 21:35 says,

---

[52] John Bowker, "The Problem of Suffering in the Qur'an," *Religious Studies* 4, no. 2 (April, 1969), 186.

[53] Ibid, 187.

[54] Cited from www.quran.com. Accessed on February 22, 2021.

[55] "Islam Beliefs: Suffering and the Problem of Evil," Patheos, accessed February 20, 2021, https://www.patheos.com/library/islam/beliefs/suffering-and-the-problem-of-evil.

[56] Cited from www.quran.com. Accessed on February 22, 2021.

> Every soul will taste death. And We test you O
> humanity with good and evil as a trial, then to Us
> you will all be returned.[57]

Here the endurance of suffering is sent from Allah to test the
faith of the one suffering.

Either view is represented in what is called a theory of
"instrumentality"—which says that suffering is meant to be an
instrument to bring about the purposes of Allah.[58] Therefore, the
practical response is to patiently endure it.

Some Muslim scholars have suggested a special form of this
endurance, which has been referred to as *rida*. This has been defined
by al-Imam al-`Izz bin Abdi-s-Salam as follows:

> *Rida* is the expansion of the heart to what has
> befallen it, its total acceptance of the divine decree
> and its not desiring to see it removed. Even though
> one may feel pain, *rida* lessens the pain because of
> the certainty and cognizance that has taken root in
> the heart. As the state of *rida* strengthens it is even
> possible that the person no longer feels pain at all.[59]

The idea is to cultivate a positive state of mind in the presence
of suffering, despite one's circumstances. Ultimately, Islam teaches
that Allah is all-powerful. Therefore, all suffering is in accordance
with his decree and will to accomplish his purposes and should be
endured in faith.

---

[57] Ibid.

[58] Bowker, "The Problem of Suffering in the Qur'an," 189.

[59] Salam, *Trials and Tribulations: Wisdom and Benefits*, (London: Daar us-
sunnah Publishers, 2004), 23-24n21. Cited in Zacharias and Vitale, *Why
Suffering?*, 125.

Judaism

As we try to understand the response from Judaism, we will see a lot of overlap with Christianity and Islam. Again, this is because all three religions hold to the existence of an all-powerful god who is in control of the universe and, therefore, to some degree allows or causes suffering. This frames the responses from these worldviews (or religions) because they have to deal with this in the context of that underlying belief. However, as noted above, we will see more overlap in the Jewish and Christian responses because the primary challenge posed by the existence of suffering will be to tenant that God is good and loving.

Now there are nuanced views within the Jewish tradition, but I think it is fair to boil the responses down to two categories. Judaism teaches that suffering is a result of individual sin or is ordained by God as a means of purification or growth.[60]

Maimonides was a twelfth-century Jewish philosopher who endorsed the view that suffering was the result of committed sins.[61] However, strictly holding to this view is difficult to reconcile with other Jewish writings (i.e., Job; Ecclesiastes 7:15), which give evidence of the suffering of the innocent.

Therefore, other Jewish scholars have proposed views that suggest suffering is a form of divine purification that ultimately brings one closer to God.[62] This purification can be in the form of a test to see if one can obey God and prove his or her faith, and it can also be a trial meant to increase a person's compassion toward the suffering of other human beings.[63] And still others hold that the ultimate reason for suffering is unknowable.

---

[60] "Suffering," Jewish Concepts, Jewish Virtual Library, accessed March 3, 2021, https://www.jewishvirtuallibrary.org/suffering.

[61] Ibid.

[62] Ibid.

[63] "Good, evil and suffering." Religious Studies: Good and evil—Unit 1, BBC, accessed March 3, 2021, https://www.bbc.co.uk/bitesize/guides/

For example, Rabbi Joseph B. Soloveitchik poses a slightly different spin on the problem of evil and suffering in his essay *Kol Dodi Dofek* (*It Is the Voice of My Beloved That Knocketh*).[64] He presents the argument that understanding God's purposes for allowing evil and suffering are beyond us. Therefore, the human endeavor should rather focus on what our response to the reality of evil and suffering should be. This shift in understanding leads him to develop a response from Jewish law, or the *halakha*.

Soloveitchik writes the following:

> The *halakha* is concerned with this problem [that of the existence of evil and suffering] as it is concerned with other problems of permitted and forbidden, liability and exemption. We do not inquire about the hidden ways of the Almighty, but rather about the path wherein man shall walk when suffering strikes.[65]

Put more simply, Soloveitchik's argument asks, "What obligation does suffering impose?"[66] This line of reasoning ultimately leads him to conclude, "Afflictions come to elevate a person, to purify and sanctify his spirit ... the function of suffering is to mend that which is flawed in an individual's personality."[67] From this purification of the individual personality, Soloveitchik argues, compassion will also

---

z7qxvcw/revision/4.

[64] "Kol Dodi Dofek." Translation published in *Theological and Halakhic Reflections on the Holocaust*, ed. Fred Heuman and Bernhard Rosenberg (Hoboken, NJ: Ktav Publishing House, 1992). Cited in Moshe Sokol, "Is There a 'Halakhic' Response to the Problem of Evil?" *The Harvard Theological Review* 92, no. 3 (July 1999):313.

[65] "Kol Dodi Dofek," 56. Cited in Sokol, "Is There a 'Halakhic' Response to the Problem of Evil?", 315–316.

[66] Ibid, 315

[67] Ibid, 316

grow and lead people to act on that compassion to relieve suffering in the world.

Nonetheless, regardless of the underlying philosophical reasoning behind suffering, the Jewish response to suffering seems to be to instruct one to endure suffering when they experience it, to relieve suffering when they see it, and to trust God with the reason for suffering—even if it is unknown.

Panentheism

Panentheism is a philosophy that has a subtle twist on the concept of god that has some resemblance to pantheism (not only in spelling!) and classical theism. Panentheism can be defined as "all in god."[68] This is very similar to pantheism (see below) but has a distinct difference. In panentheism, the world is still distinct from god but is part of god. The conception of god, according to panentheism, is similar to classical theism in that god is viewed as the greatest possible being. However, panentheism sees that god as the totality of all that is possible.[69]

This conceptualization of god fundamentally shifts the way the universe is viewed. This form of panentheism (known as modal panentheism) sees the universe as consisting of an infinite number of possible worlds, such that every possible world does, in fact, exist—we just happen to find ourselves in this world where the evil we see exists in the way that it does. For example, Yujin Nagasawa writes,

> The problem of evil for modal panentheism is more intractable than the problem of evil for pantheism. While pantheism entails only the thesis that

---

[68] Geisler, "Panentheism" in *The Big Book of Christian Apologetics*, 421.

[69] Yujin Nagasawa, "Chapter 5: Modal Panentheism," in *Alternative concepts of God: essays on the metaphysics of the divine*, ed. Andrei A. Buckareff and Yujin Nagasawa (New York: Oxford University Press, 2016), 1.

all *actual* instances of evil are (i.e., all instances of evil in the actual world) part of God, modal panentheism entails the much stronger thesis that all *possible* instances of evil (i.e., all instances of evil in all possible worlds), including the very worst possible instances of evil, are part of God. This means that modal panentheism entails that there is, as part of God, a state of affairs in which, for example, millions of innocent children are tortured for an extended period, possibly eternally, for no reason.[70]

This view espouses then that pain and suffering exist in this world because it must exist in some possible world. This view of god claims that all possible forms of evil will exist anyway, because all possible states of affairs will exist in some possible world. Thus, the reason we see or experience the pain and suffering around us is because we happen to be in the "possible world" in which that form of suffering exists, but all forms of suffering must exist in some possible world as "part of god."[71]

Pantheism

Pantheism teaches that "god is all in all."[72] This view sees all of the material world (including us) as extensions of the divine. All pantheists believe that god and the world are one, but there are differences among pantheists to explain how this works. Nonetheless, this view of oneness ultimately leads to the inability to make meaningful distinctions, including any distinction between good and evil.[73] If

---

[70] Ibid, 10-11.

[71] Ibid, 11.

[72] Geisler, "Pantheism" in *The Big Book of Christian Apologetics,* 425.

[73] Jeyachandran. "Challenges from Eastern Religions," *Beyond Opinion,* 103.

there is no distinction between good and evil, pantheists are forced to conclude that our perception of good and evil must, therefore, be illusory. For example, Christian Science[74] holds to a form of pantheism that teaches that matter, evil, sickness, and death are not real and simply illusions of the mind.[75]

This sort of belief seems to instruct people toward an attitude of apathy in their approach to the reality of suffering in our world. Believing that suffering is illusory encourages us to "not think about it" or ignore it. That appears to be the conclusion reached by those holding pantheistic views when we see statements like this: "All apparent evil is the result of ignorance, and will disappear to the degree that it is no longer thought about, believed in or indulged in."[76]

Pluralism

Pluralism affirms that reality is "found in many."[77] Essentially, this view says that there are many expressions of reality that are all equally true. This makes the response to the problem of evil and suffering from this viewpoint rather easy to explain. Pluralism would maintain that all of the above explanations for the existence of evil

---

[74] Note that although the term *Christian* is used here, the central teachings of Christian Science deny many (if not all!) of the core doctrines of biblical Christianity. Therefore, this view should not be confused with the beliefs expressed under the section on Christianity described above.

[75] Mary Baker Eddy. *Miscellaneous Writings*. (Boston: Christian Science Publishing Society, 1896), 27. Cited from Ronald Rhodes. "Tough Questions about Evil." In *Who Made God?* ed. Ravi Zacharias and Norman Geisler (Grand Rapids, MI: Zondervan, 2003), 40.

[76] Ernest Holmes, *What Religious Science Teaches* (Los Angeles: Science of Mind Publications, 1974), 13. Cited in Rhodes, "Tough Questions about Evil," 40.

[77] Geisler, "Pluralism" in *The Big Book of Christian Apologetics*, 442.

and suffering are equally and simultaneously true. Which view you choose to believe and function under is up to you.

As we can see, there are multiple ways that people have tried to answer the question "Why do we hurt?" and we end up with different answers. Atheism says, "There is no reason." Agnosticism says, "We don't know the reason." Buddhism says, "The reason is your own desires." Dualism says, "The reason is that the principle of evil is being expressed in the world." Hinduism says, "The reason is your own evil deeds." Islam says, "The reason is it is Allah's will." Judaism says, "We may not know the reason, but we ought to do something about it." Panentheism says, "The reason is because it is part of god." Pantheism says, "There is no real problem." And pluralism says, "The reason is all of the above."

Can we see how the results of these different paradigms lead to a problem as to what the ultimate solution is? The Buddhist response to cease from desiring won't necessarily help the problem if it is *karma* being expressed in one's life. Likewise, if the reason for suffering is that it is "part of god," then any attempts to do anything about it are futile. What paradigm we adopt will influence the strategy we employ to address the suffering and pain that we see in the world around us. We see that the reality of pain presents us with a paradigm problem. That is, which one is correct?

And what complicates this matter further is that not only does the paradigm we live under have to answer the question "Why do we hurt?" but it also has to answer fundamental questions like "Where did we come from?" and "Why are we here?" and "What is it that establishes right and wrong?" and "What happens after we die?" and "If there is a god, how are we to know that god?" So when we are evaluating all of these different paradigms, we must consider not only how they answer the problem of pain but also what they say about these other questions. As my intention here is not to develop and describe the entirety of the Christian worldview but only to address a specific question that is often posed to that belief system, I am simply going to say that I believe the Christian response presents the most comprehensive, compassionate, and livable answers to these questions—and specifically to the question "Why do we hurt?" And I would like to invite you to read on in this book to discover why I believe that.

In doing this, our first stop will be to confront the strongest challenge to the Christian response to the presence of pain and suffering in the world. That is, "How can a good and loving God allow so much pain and suffering?" This is the philosophical problem posed to Christianity.

3

The Philosophical Problem

The day started like a typical Tuesday for me. Sitting at my usual workstation in the Biomechanics Lab, earbuds in, Pandora blasting theme scores from my favorite movies, and spreadsheets of data before me! As my tunnel vision was setting in, I heard a faint voice in the background ...

"Can I ask you random question?" One of the graduate students had quietly walked over to me, ripping me out of my time warp of concentration.

"Uh, I guess so. What's up?" I answered, feeling a little confused.

"You're a Christian, right?"

"Yeah ..." I answered somewhat hesitatingly, as I was completely uncertain of where this was going.

"How do you do it?"

"Do what?" I asked. At this point, I was totally baffled and had no idea what this student was getting at.

"How can you believe in a God who says that He is loving when all this [insert explicative here] is going on?"

Although not everyone will ask the question so clearly or so passionately, this is the question that most of us have wrestled with to some degree. When asked what question people would ask God if they could, the most frequent answer was "Why is there pain and suffering in the world?"[78]

Although many people struggle with wondering why there is so much pain in the world, interestingly enough, it seems that they always direct their confusion, frustration, and, oftentimes, anger toward God. Regardless of the person's religion or belief system, there is no hesitation to put God in the blocks and unleash our opinions and judgments upon Him. But you don't hear anybody letting loose an emotional tirade against Gaia or Mother Earth. Nor do you hear many people just shrugging their shoulders at the issue and saying, "Well, that's just natural selection. The world is purging itself of the weak."

The problem of pain is almost always posed as a philosophical problem for those who believe in a god—especially the God described in the Christian faith. Renowned theologian and preacher John Stott has been quoted as declaring the existence of suffering as "the single greatest challenge to the Christian faith."[79] This is such a challenge because when no satisfying or concrete answer is found, this can cause people to walk away because of an apparent contradiction, inconsistency, or false belief in the faith. Or (and?) the lack of reasoned answers gives ammunition to detractors to criticize the Christian faith. Yet like we saw in the first chapter, given how pervasive pain and suffering is in our world, this question—this problem—is crying out for an answer. It is the question of our day and age, "How can there be a good and loving God when there is so much evil, pain, and suffering in the world?"

So, in answering it, we must see the full context of both the question and the person asking it.

---

[78] "The OmniPoll," Barna Research Group, Ltd. January, 1999. Cited in Lee Strobel, *The Case for Faith* (Grand Rapids, MI: Zondervan, 2000), 30.
[79] Strobel, *The Case for Faith*, 57

"Oof! That's a huge question," I responded to the student that fateful day in the lab. "But it's a fair one! I've wrestled with it myself. Tell me more about why you are asking though. Is there something specific that happened recently that is prompting the question? What's going on that you are asking me this now?"

"I just can't handle it anymore!" he said with a tone of exasperation. "We are studying and learning about all these injuries, illnesses, and diseases in school and how to help people through it. But I keep imagining all the pain that comes along with those conditions. I have always believed in God, but I just don't understand how He can let all this happen if He really is as powerful and loving as Christians always say He is."

"Ah, I see," I said as I was beginning to understand the context of his question. "You are not alone in wondering about this. This question has been wrestled with by a lot of people! But I would be happy to tell you how I have come to understand how this works ..."

To be clear, this was not a one-time conversation where I systematically listed off knock-down arguments for Christianity, and he walked away, hands raised, shouting, "Hallelujah!" No. This was just the first of many conversations with this brave student. Some of them I think I really helped. Some of them I think I missed his question and just soapboxed at him. But over the course of several months, talking through a few different books together and a lot of prayer, the Lord moved and enlightened his understanding. For that, I am grateful and so happy that I got to play a part in this young man's journey in seeking God and finding His Son, Jesus.

But this is not a recent phenomenon. It's not a question that people of our generation have just now started asking. This challenge has been around for centuries, and one of the most famous forms of the question was put forth by the Greek philosopher Epicurus sometime around 300 BC. Now, some[80] claim that Epicurus formed this as a challenge to God's providence, not His existence, and that this was never used as an argument for atheism until the seventeenth or eighteenth century. But whether this was put forth as an argument for atheism by David Hume, Jean Paul Sartre, Bertrand Russell, or your aunt Lucy doesn't really matter. The point is people have been pondering this for a long time. Nonetheless, Epicurus is usually the one credited as having articulated the original line of thought, and thus this challenge has been referred to as the *Epicurean paradox*.

It goes like this:[81]

> If God is willing to prevent evil (suffering) but not able, then He is not all-powerful.
> If God is able to prevent evil (suffering) but not willing, then He is not good.
> But if God is both willing and able, how can evil (suffering) exist?
> If God is neither able nor willing, why call Him God?

At first glance, we might feel flattened and smashed by this challenge, but let's take a moment to really look at this paradox. Does this argument actually work? Does it pass tests of logic and reasoning? Currently, the consensus among philosophers—atheist, agnostic, and theist—is no.

Essentially, what this line of questioning is trying to say is that, "It is impossible (logically) for God *and* suffering to exist at the same time." It is the third point that reveals this mostly clearly. This statement is saying that God, as we know Him (all-powerful and all good), and suffering cannot exist simultaneously. We are using

---

[80] e.g. Christian Hofrieter, "Situating the Question," Lecture 1.2 in Why Suffering? Ravi Zacharias Academy, February, 2020.

[81] Adapted from "Suffering and Evil: The Logical Problem," Videos, Reasonable Faith, https://www.reasonablefaith.org/videos/short-videos/suffering-and-evil-the-logical-problem/.

the term *suffering* here instead of evil because we could argue that suffering is the *felt* outcome of evil. Suffering is the thing that we can see, feel, and experience as a result of there being evil in the world.

But right away we can see that this question poses different problems. A logical one—is it really *impossible* for God and suffering to exist together? An evidential one—or is it just *improbable* that God and suffering exist together? And an emotional one—it doesn't *feel right* that God and suffering exist together.[82] The emotional problem is arguably the hardest to deal with, because it is one that we experience and struggle with at a basic human level since we rightly *feel* the injustice and inhumanity of many forms of suffering. But as William Lane Craig has astutely pointed out, an emotional argument only allows us to *reject* God's existence on this line of reasoning. We have to look at the logical and evidential problems and evaluate their validity in order to *refute* God's existence.[83]

So let's start by looking at the logical problem. Is it *impossible* for God and suffering to both exist? The short answer here is no; there is no logical incompatibility in this statement. Even the well-known atheist J. L. Mackie admits this. "We can concede that the problem of evil does not, after all, show that the central doctrines of theism are logically inconsistent with one another."[84]

But I think it will be helpful to walk through this step by step to see where and how the logic breaks down. We can rearrange Epicurus's line of questioning into a more formal series of statements to help us see this. With a little rearranging, the paradox can be summarized into an argument like this:[85]

---

[82] William Lane Craig, *On Guard: Defending your Faith with Reason and Precision* (Colorado Springs, CO: David C Cook, 2010), 152.

[83] Ibid, 153

[84] J. L. Mackie, *The Miracle of Theism: Arguments for and against the existence of God* (Oxford: Oxford University Press, 1982), 154.

[85] Adapted from Craig, *On guard: Defending Your Faith with Reason and Precision*, 154.

1. It is logically impossible for God and suffering to both exist.
2. Suffering does exist.
3. Therefore, God does not exist.

If both statements one and two are shown to be true, then the conclusion logically follows that God does not exist. Now, at first glance, this seems like it would be hard to refute. But we have to look very closely at the first statement. Is this really true? For this to be logically impossible, God and suffering must be shown to be contradictory, either explicitly or implicitly.[86]

Well, there is no explicit contradiction here. A frequently used example of an explicit contradiction is a married bachelor. These two terms refer to different descriptions of a man that cannot be true of the same man at the same time. If he is married, by definition he cannot be a bachelor. Likewise, if he is a bachelor, by definition he cannot be married. The terms contradict each other. For our purposes here, a contradiction would be *God exists, and there is no God*. The statement "it is logically impossible for God and suffering to both exist" is clearly not explicitly contradictory. So then we have to ask, is there some kind of contradiction that is implicit in this statement? Stated otherwise, must we infer *necessarily* that if God exists that suffering does not exist?

First let's review what a necessary inference is. An inference is a conclusion that we draw when we aren't provided all of the information, but we have bits of information that help us answer a question. But what's important to note is that from the information we have, for our answer to be *necessary*, it must be an irresistible answer—there can't be another option. There can't be any other potential explanations or conclusions. For example, a necessary inference would look like this:

1. All men can grow beards.

---

[86] Ibid, 155.

2. John is a man.
3. Therefore, John can grow a beard.

Now, we can argue whether or not point number one is true—how one defines the ability to grow a beard is a matter of interpretation! But it is easy to see how, given both statements one and two are true, the conclusion follows *necessarily*—it must be that way.

For an argument to be shown as definitively true, the inference has to be necessary. But we can still use our reason to arrive at conclusions that are probably true. This is called *sufficient* inference, or *reasonable* inference. Let's look at another example closer to home in Christian theology to see an example of this. The use of inference is how we arrive at the doctrine of the Trinity. Now we can argue if this is necessary or sufficient inference, but the fact that there is uncertainty surrounding classifying it justifies it as an appropriate example (I think).[87]

1. The Bible says there is one God (Deuteronomy 6:4).
2. The Bible describes God through three persons (Matthew 28:19).
3. Therefore, one God exists as a being consisting of three persons (a Trinity).

Statement one limits God's quantity, while statement two describes an aspect of His nature. Neither statement alone gives a full description of God. But assuming both are true, we can take them together and arrive at a fuller understanding of God. We can

---

[87] For the sake of clarity, let me state explicitly that in no way am I trying to cast doubt on the doctrine of the Trinity. I am using this simply as an example of how we use inference in the formation of Christian doctrine. Also, although I think the way the argument is phrased here qualifies as a sufficient inference, when we take the sum total of biblical teaching and evidence, the doctrine of the Trinity becomes more and more evident.

conclude statement three, because to conclude otherwise would call in to question either statement one or two. So, at the very least, this qualifies as a sufficient inference, even if someone is hesitant to say it is a necessary one.

Now, if we apply that reasoning to our question of God and suffering, we can then ask, "Is the *necessary* inference of God's existence that suffering can't exist?"

Now, that is not obvious from the statement itself, so there must be hidden assumptions.

What are those then?

Combining the work of William Lane Craig[88] and Vince Vitale,[89] we can identify at least five assumptions:

1. Suffering (or evil) does exist.
2. God is all-powerful and, therefore, can create any world He wants.
3. God is loving and, therefore, prefers a world without suffering.
4. We should know what God's reasons are for allowing suffering.
5. Our lives will be lived in a world of suffering.

To say that God can't exist because of so much evil and suffering in the world is really a very loaded statement because the person is smuggling in all five of these assumptions—if not more! At this point, let's return to the question we are evaluating: is it logically impossible for God and suffering to both exist?

In order for this to be a necessary inference, it must also be shown that all five of these assumptions are true and consistent with one another with no possible alternatives or explanations for how God could exist even in the presence of suffering.

[88] Craig, *On guard. Defending Your Faith with Reason and Precision*, 155-157.
[89] Vitale, "Questioning the question." Lecture 2.2—Why Suffering? Ravi Zacharias Academy. February, 2020.

Now, we are going to touch on each of these assumptions, and we will find that the necessity of this line of reasoning breaks down at assumption two (and objections can be raised to the remaining three as well!).

In looking at the first assumption, you're probably thinking, *Of course suffering and evil exist! Just look at the world around us! And didn't I just read an entire chapter demonstrating that?* To which I will say, "Yes, I totally agree!" However, just like we saw in the last chapter, there are some worldviews in our culture that actually deny the existence of suffering, evil, or both.

Remember pantheism is one example of this. And, arguably, atheism is another view that has difficulty providing an argument for the reality of evil (although I don't know that any would deny suffering).[90] So we do actually need to substantiate that evil and suffering are real things!

But even though there are some worldviews that deny the existence of suffering (and evil), I think most people you come across will readily acknowledge that suffering is a reality of the world we live in.

So, let's grant assumption one and move on to assumption two: God is all-powerful and, therefore, can create any world He wants. Well, this is true in the sense that God is all-powerful. The Christian view of God is that He possesses an attribute known as *omnipotence*, which literally means "all-powerful." This is often understood as His ability to complete "all of His will."[91] I include this definition

---

[90] Because of this, if the question "How can a good and loving God allow evil and suffering?" is being posed by an atheist, one can actually flip the question back on him by asking, "On what basis can you claim that this or that is evil?" Our ability to make a moral judgment on the tragedies in this world is actually evidence found in one of the most compelling arguments *for* God's existence—not against it. This is known as the *moral argument*, which is quite compelling!

[91] See Wayne Grudem, *Systematic Theology: An Introduction to Biblical Doctrine* (Grand Rapids, MI: Zondervan, 1994), 216.

to clarify that we don't believe that God can do "whatever He chooses" in an absolute sense. For example, the Bible tells us that "it is impossible for God to lie" (Hebrews 6:18), and this is because "He cannot deny Himself" (2 Timothy 2:13 NASB). So God cannot do things that contradict His nature, because if God is truth (see John 14:6), then if He were ever to lie in any way, He would cease to possess the attribute of truthfulness and faithfulness in its ultimate sense. Essentially, He would cease being God if He were to lie.

So there are two assumptions being made in this second statement. The first is that the world God wants is one without suffering. And second, that such a world can be made without God contradicting His nature. In responding to this, we can raise several challenges. For example, can we assume that the world God wants is one without pain? What if pain and suffering serve an instrumental purpose in shaping His world, such as crafting and shaping beings who can love? What if He wanted to create persons who can love not only Him but also their fellow humans? Then is it possible for God to make a world with persons who can love, while not limiting some aspect of their freedom?

With that list of rhetorical questions, let's start with what is probably the most common response to this assumption that you will encounter among Christians. The idea is presented by proposing that for love to be possible, some degree of freedom must be granted. This is usually referred to as *free will*, and this argument in response to the challenge to God's existence from evil and suffering is known as the *free will defense*. This has been thoroughly developed by Alvin Plantinga in his book *God, Freedom, and Evil*,[92] and modifications of and objections to this argument have been presented by John S. Feinberg in his work, *The Many Faces of Evil*.[93] So I am only going to provide a summary here.

---

[92] Alvin Plantinga, *God, Freedom, and Evil*. (Grand Rapids, MI: Eerdmans Publishing Company, 1974. Reprinted in 2001).

[93] John S. Feinberg, *The Many Faces of Evil: Theological Systems and The Problems of Evil* (Wheaton, IL: Crossway, 2004).

The argument goes like this: In order for love to be possible, there must be free will from which beings can choose to love. That's because for something to be considered love, we think of that as something born out of a free choice, right? Coercion, manipulation, and determination are not typically words we associate with the concept of love. Rather, love is said to be realized in the context of being able to willingly give one's life to something, or someone, out of gratitude, devotion, and affection.

So if people are free to do as they choose, there is inherently the possibility of people choosing to do what they want—to choose to serve themselves rather than others. People may choose to stray from God's will or to outright disobey God. They may choose to be kind or unkind. They may choose to act in love or to reject love. When there is free will, there is the freedom to choose. If there is the freedom to choose, there is the possibility of people doing things maliciously and inflicting harm. The *possibility* of evil, pain, and suffering is a potential outcome of free will, and free will seems to be a component of love.

Therefore, if free will is necessary for love to be possible, then if God desired a world with beings who can love, He then may allow the potential for evil and suffering to make possible a world where there are beings capable of love. The evil, pain, and suffering we experience in the world is then the result of the free actions of the beings (i.e., people) God has made. This offers a potential explanation that undercuts assumption two. Therefore, the argument fails.

But I know someone is thinking right now, *If God is all-powerful, couldn't He just make people want to choose to love Him and others?* If we say He can't, doesn't that mean He isn't all-powerful? Well, this leads us into a very deep discussion regarding the compatibility of God's sovereignty and the human will, what degree of freedom our will has, and in what areas of life. A full treatment of that topic is way beyond the scope of this book, but to summarize, there appears to be a both/and sort of tension that remains a mystery to us. God is sovereign over history; He controls it and knows its outcome. Yet people have the capacity to choose and act in accordance with their nature and therefore have responsibility for their actions.[94]

Now, is the free will defense perfect and without any limitations? No, definitely not. But I do think it provides a framework to demonstrate how God can have reasons (and moral ones at that!) for allowing evil and suffering in this the world. And if we can demonstrate that, then we have defeated the logical argument against God from the problem of suffering![95]

So, at the very least, we have already proposed a solution that disrupts the logic of necessary inference, even if we may object to this argument on grounds related to God's sovereignty, the nature of human freedom, and its role in salvation.[96] Simply because this argument is potentially true (on a philosophical level even if we could debate it on a biblical level), it works to refute the logic of the Epicurean paradox we are discussing. Nonetheless, let's keep working through our list of assumptions by asking, "Could it still be a *sufficient* inference to say that God and suffering can't exist? If it's not *impossible* for God and suffering to both exist, is it then *improbable*?"

Let's move on to the third assumption and see what happens:

---

[94] The reader is referred to John Lennox's work *Determined to Believe?* (Grand Rapids, MI: Zondervan, 2017) for an in-depth treatment of this topic. He provides a summary from various theological views and does a very thorough analysis of several passages of scripture to show this tension. One can also refer to Wayne Grudem's *Systematic Theology* in chapter 16, "God's Providence," or James White's *The Potter's Freedom* (Calvary Press Publishing, 2009) for alternative views that are equally thorough in their scope.

[95] For a more concise summary (compared to the extensive work of Feinberg) of the limitations of the free will defense and how demonstrating any moral reason for allowing evil and suffering defeats the logical problem poised against God, see Timothy Keller's *Walking with God through Pain and Suffering*, "The Problem of Evil," (New York, NY: Penguin Books, 2013).

[96] I am referring to the classic Calvinism versus Arminianism debate here with regards to the role of human freedom in salvation.

God is loving and, therefore, prefers a world without suffering. Well, how do we know that? To make such a statement is already assuming that we know something about God, His character, and His will. Further, it assumes that all suffering is bad, which is not necessarily the case. The story of Joseph is illustrative here (see Genesis 37–50). Remember, Joseph was envied by his brothers, so they sold him into slavery in Egypt. He worked his way into prominence and was then falsely accused and thrown into prison. Then many years later, because of God's granting him the ability to interpret dreams, he rises to a high position in the land of Egypt and leads them through a terrible famine. During this time, his brothers come to Egypt for help. And Joseph, when revealing his identity to his brothers and forgiving them for what they did to him, says, "You meant evil against me, but God meant it for good" (Genesis 50:20 NASB). This story shows that sometimes what appears, by our judgment, to be evil and terrible, may actually be working something deeper to bring about God's purposes (see Romans 8:28).[97]

So the assumption that God prefers a world without suffering is only true if suffering is capricious, serves no purpose, and is done outside of a loving intention. But if suffering is intentionally allowed for the specific purpose of bringing about something good, can't this still be understood as something that is occurring within the confines of love?

We can all think of examples of this, right? Think of having a cavity filled or a tumor removed—painful procedures that we gladly undergo to avoid a later outcome that is *really* bad. So if we all agree that a dentist or surgeon can do something that causes pain to bring about good, isn't the same true of God? But since God is infinitely more powerful and wise than a dentist or surgeon, can't He use means on a much grander scale to bring about the good He

---

[97] In one sense, what I think this implies is that God is sovereign over evil. Only He has the ability and prerogative to take something evil and use it for good.

intends, even if from our perspective it seems harsh, mean, cruel, or even evil? In other words, if suffering has a divine purpose that is rooted in love, then can't God still be loving even though He allows suffering to exist in accordance with His divine decree?[98]

Here is another response to the existence of pain and suffering. So if you have some issues with the free will defense proposed earlier, don't worry. I've got you covered. This view is more in line with a Reformed understanding of God's sovereignty. It essentially says that whatever evil occurs on earth has been ordained by God to occur to bring about His purposes. Wayne Grudem summarizes this position well:

> In approaching this question [What is the relationship between God and evil in the world?], it is best first to read the passages of Scripture that most directly address it. We can begin by looking at several passages that affirm that God did, indeed, cause evil events to come about and evil deeds to be done. But we must remember that in all these passages it is very clear that Scripture nowhere shows God *as directly doing anything evil*, but rather as bringing about evil deeds through the willing actions of moral creatures. Moreover, *Scripture never blames God for evil or shows God as taking pleasure in evil*, and Scripture never excuses human beings for the wrong they do. However we understand God's relationship to evil, we must *never* come to the point where we think that we are not responsible for the

---

[98] For example, the *Westminster Larger Catechism*, in defining the decrees of God in Question 12, states: "God's decrees are the wise, free, and holy decisions from the purposes of his will. By them, from all eternity and for his own glory, he has unchangeably foreordained everything that happens in time, and particularly those things that involve angels and human beings."

evil that we do, or that God takes pleasure in evil
or is to be blamed for it.[99]

This approach uses what is known as *concurrence*.[100] This means
that God uses the acts and intentions of people to bring about His
purposes. In other words, the actions of people are their own, but
God has ordained those actions in such a way that He is working
through the willful actions of those people. If we apply this to the
existence of evil and suffering, concurrence would propose that in
His infinite wisdom and knowledge, God allows humans to make
willing choices that are evil, but He allows this only in so much as
they bring about His good and loving purposes. That is to say that
God can ordain the willing and evil choices and actions of people,
knowing that He will use those actions to ultimately bring about
His good and loving purposes and His own glory. And the ultimate
example of this is the crucifixion of Jesus Christ. Look at what we
read in Acts 2:23 (NASB):

> This Man [Jesus], delivered over by the predetermined
> plan and foreknowledge of God, you nailed to a cross
> by the hands of godless men and put Him to death.

The torture and murder of the only sinless man to have ever
walked the earth (an act of evil resulting in human suffering)
happened according to the "predetermined plan and foreknowledge
of God" but was done "by the hands of godless men." God worked
an unbelievable good (the atonement and forgiveness of the sins of
humans) through an act of evil (the murder of an innocent man)!
Certainly, the correct response to this is to echo Paul in his doxology:

---

[99] Grudem, *Systematic Theology*. Chapter 16: "God's Providence," 323.
[100] For a fuller discussion of this idea see Grudem's *Systematic Theology* pages
317–331.

> Oh, the depth of the riches of the wisdom and knowledge of God! How unsearchable his judgments, and his paths beyond tracing out! Who has known the mind of the Lord? Or who has been his counselor? Who has ever given to God, that God should repay him? For from him and through him and to him are all things. To him be the glory forever! Amen. (Romans 11:33–36)

What we see here is that as long as God, who is good, loving, just, righteous, and holy, has sufficient reason to allow evil in this world, He may *prefer* to allow it to happen. All we need to do then is demonstrate what *one* purpose may be, and we can think of several: He may allow this suffering to build and grow and mature the souls of humans,[101] He may allow evil and suffering because to not do so would fundamentally change the nature of the beings He made to reflect His image,[102] or He may allow evil and suffering because it brings Him glory to save His creation from evil and to bring justice and wrath upon evil (see Romans 9:22–23).[103] I will go on in subsequent chapters to describe other reasons that God may allow suffering in this world, so stay tuned!

But as soon as we can demonstrate a potential reason that God may allow suffering, it immediately disrupts the logic of this statement, and, again, the logical problem of evil is defeated at assumption three,

---

[101] Here I have in mind an idea similar to the "Soul-Building Theodicy" of John Hicks as described in Feinburg's *The Many Faces of Evil*, pages 142–146.

[102] This is how I would summarize (accurately I hope!) the view put forth by John Feinburg in chapter 6, "God and Moral Evil," in *The Many Faces of Evil*.

[103] This idea is super challenging to think about, but one I think we often forget is a possible explanation for why God allows evil, pain, and suffering. One day His good and righteous judgment on these things will be put on display for all to see.

and we build up further evidence that casts doubt on the evidential problem—the evidence is, in fact, stacking up in favor of God![104]

At this point, I imagine the thought on the minds of many is, *Do we know which option is ultimately* the *reason that God has allowed evil and suffering?* No, I don't think so. But let me ask this question: "Why do we assume that we should know the reason that God allows suffering? Why do we think that we are privy to such information?"

This is assumption four: we should know what God's reasons are for allowing suffering. Well, should we? Can we? Do we have any right or basis to believe this? We can't even predict the weather forecast for the weekend with anything close to infallible accuracy; what makes us think we can predict the purposes for human suffering on a cosmic scale?

To maintain any degree of academic integrity, we all must acknowledge the limitations of our human reasoning. If you read any scientific publications, there is an entire section devoted to the limitations of the study, project, model, or technique. The fact of the matter is that we, as humans, are limited in time, space, and knowledge, and therefore, we cannot assume that we do know, or will know, all (or any for that matter) of the reasons that God may allow suffering.[105]

---

[104] This is particularly true when we consider all of the biblical evidence for God's existence (such as the internal consistency of the Bible, fulfilled prophecy in Christ, and the lives its teachings have transformed), the philosophical evidence for God's existence (such as evidence from the universe's beginning and design as well as from the existence of moral values and duties), and that all worldviews need to answer other questions about ultimate reality, such as origin, morality, purpose, and destiny. When all those things are considered, this one objection to God's existence—the presence of evil and suffering in the world—does not surmount the evidence in favor of the God of the Christian faith. This is especially true when we consider the Christian response to the question as we are dealing with it now!

[105] Although we are grateful that God, in His grace, does reveal aspects of His will and His reasons to us, I believe that He has revealed more than enough

And this is helpful for Christians to remember. We don't have to expect that we can fully answer this question for everyone. If you don't feel you have a great answer to the why of pain and suffering in a particular case, that's OK! We won't always have one.

How can I say that? Isn't the point of this book to answer the question of why? Well, yes, it is—but only to provide a potential why, not a universal—or ultimate—one.[106] And this is an important distinction. I say this because when we consider this biblically, the answer is clear that we should *not* assume that we will know, or that we should know, what all of God's reasons are for allowing suffering in each and every situation.

There are several passages that clearly teach on the limited understanding of humans. Deuteronomy 29:29 (NASB) says, "The secret things belong to the Lord our God, but the things revealed belong to us." This implies that there are some things that *will* be kept secret from us. There *will* be aspects of God's will and purposes that are not going to be revealed to us here on earth. First Corinthians 13:9 clarifies this further when we read, "We know in part." In Isaiah 55:8–9, God says,

> "For my thoughts are not your thoughts, neither are
> your ways my ways," declares the LORD. "As the
> heavens are higher than the earth, so are my ways

---

that we can trust Him and have confidence that He does have good reasons for allowing evil and suffering in the ways that He does even if we don't know precisely what those reasons are.

[106] What I mean here is that God may be working different things in different situations among different people and therefore may have different reasons for allowing pain and suffering in different circumstances, so our task is to reason through—biblically—what He says some of those reasons may be and then apply them to our situation. And all the details of specific circumstances may not allow us to know the why. We will get to this through the story of Job in chapter 6. But in an ultimate sense, as in "Why does God allow suffering at all?" I don't think we are given a full answer other than it works in us a fuller understanding of God's nature, love, and glory.

higher than your ways and my thoughts than your
thoughts."

We see that in Old Testament and New Testament alike; both
teach that we have limited understanding and that we will *not* know
all of the ways and reasons of God. Now, don't take this to mean
that I am suggesting that you take a "the Bible says it, I believe
it, that settles it"[107] approach with no further explanation of your
reasoning. If someone is honestly asking questions regarding how
to reconcile pain and suffering with a belief in God, we should hear
those questions and engage in the discussion. I *am* saying that we
will reach a point, or confront a situation, where we must step back
and say, "Lord, I just don't understand this. I don't get it. I don't
know why you are allowing this. But I do know that you love us,
and I trust you." So it's OK if we can't answer everything, because
we won't be able to.

And lastly, assumption five: we will live in a world filled with
suffering. Now, I wanted to bring this into the discussion because I
think this allows us to consider an essential point. Acknowledging
that the world we live in now is filled with pain, suffering, and evil
really only becomes a challenge if we believe that this life—this
world—is all that there is. If we think that a death here is just a
life being snuffed out, that seems harsh. It seems like that person
has missed out on all that this life has to offer. But if we remember
that the life we live on earth is only a blip in eternity and that we
have a hope of new heavens, new earth, and new life that awaits us,
that should change our perspective. Instead of asking why did that
person's life end before its full potential? In light of eternity, isn't it

---

[107] Although it certainly is true that if the Bible says it, we should believe it,
and that should settle it, I would encourage winsome explanations as to why
that is true.

just as reasonable to ask, why did that person get the express ticket to heaven? Why did he or she get to leave this broken planet already?[108]

If you are a Christian, we cannot evaluate the suffering in our life—or in any one else's life—only in the context of this world. We must remember that there is an eternal perspective to this as well, and we do well to set our minds on it (see Colossians 3:1). And when we do that, it becomes a little easier to cry out with the apostle Paul, "For momentary, light affliction is producing for us an eternal weight of glory far beyond all comparison" (2 Corinthians 4:17 NASB) and "to die is gain" (Philippians 1:21). So, yes, there is suffering now, but we eagerly await the coming of God's kingdom where "He will wipe away every tear from [our] eyes. There will be no more death or mourning or crying or pain, for the old order of things has passed away" (Revelation 21:4).

So lest I philosophize us so deep that we all drown, let's pivot here and come up for air. What I hope I have made abundantly clear is that the existence of evil, pain, and suffering does not make the existence of God impossible; nor does it make belief in God irrational. This challenge does not pass tests of logic. It is not contradictory. It is not a necessary inference. And we can show that it is not even a sufficient inference. We *cannot* say that it is impossible for God and suffering to exist simultaneously. The logical problem is defeated.

What about the evidential problem? Is it still improbable that God and suffering both exist? I hope that, given the potential solutions we just looked at, it is looking actually quite probable that God has good reasons for allowing suffering, and He does in fact reveal what some of those reasons are.

---

[108] This statement is not meant to be harsh or to imply that we shouldn't care about what happens in this world. Suffering, pain, loss, sadness, and grief are real things, and it is critical to understand that. I am simply trying to point out that the person who believes in eternity can (and should) have a heavenly perspective. That is, we should view things in light of what we know about the hope of heaven (see Colossians 3:1–3).

Considering that, let's just reason together a little further. What if God and suffering do both exist? How do we reconcile that? As a Christian, how can I explain that? We have seen that there are plenty of intellectual ways we can defend this, but how do we do it biblically? What does the Bible actually say about this? Because that's what really matters, isn't it?

First, the Bible clearly acknowledges the existence of God. The very first verse in the Bible says, "In the beginning, *God* ..." This is an emphatic statement of His existence.

The Bible also acknowledges the existence of evil. Within the creation narrative, we are told of the tree of the knowledge of good and *evil* (Genesis 2:17). In Ecclesiastes, we are told that "the hearts of men, moreover, are full of *evil*" (Ecclesiastes 9:3). And Jesus tells us that out of the heart come *evil* thoughts (Mark 7:21). So God and evil both exist in this world.

The Bible then teaches that God desired a world where man existed to bear His image. Genesis 1:27 says, "God created man in his own image." Then, since God is love (1 John 4:8), part of being made in God's image is having the capacity to reflect that love. And in order to love, we must willingly make choices that reveal the object of that love. Those choices are often made in accordance with our desires (which reflect our will). And our will is expressive of the nature of our being. Therefore, we make real choices that are consistent with our nature. And to reflect the love of God, ultimately, is for a man to willingly choose to "lay down his life for his friends" (John 15:13; see also 1 John 3:16). This will also play out in a practical way in our everyday experiences by each of us making choices that reflect the object of our affections (i.e., love). Like Joshua tells the people of Israel, "*Choose* for yourselves today whom you will serve" (Joshua 24:15 NASB; emphasis mine). However, every time we are considering the choices we make, we have to remember that all of us have been corrupted by sin and therefore have a sinful nature and make choices that are expressive of that. The existence of people who make choices according to their nature (a nature that is corrupted by sin) makes possible the doing of evil and leads to, at least some of, the pain and suffering we see in the world.[109]

The Bible also teaches that we will not know all of the reasons that God allows this pain and suffering to continue as long as it does (see Deuteronomy 29:29; 1 Corinthians 13:9), but it does say that part of the reason is that God is allowing as many people as possible to be saved. Look at what we read in 2 Peter 3:9 (NASB):

> The Lord is not slow about His promise, as some count slowness, but is patient toward you, not

---

[109] The astute theologian or Bible scholar may react to my avoidance of the term *freedom* in this explanation. I defer from that term as it will likely trigger other issues surrounding doctrines regarding *election*. My intention here is not to enter into that debate but only to show that humans do have some capacity to love and to choose. That seems clear from the Bible, seems apparent in our daily experience in making choices every day, and the fact that even Christians still sin—they choose to disobey God at times. These choices appear to be *free* in the sense that they are made without *direct* interference from God (e.g., we are not puppets on strings). However, this does not make us free in the sense that we are in control of our destiny but does make us free to make choices in accordance with what we *want*. The problem is our nature is corrupted in such a way that what we want is often sinful. Romans 6:20 actually describes us as being "slaves to sin," thus the will of humans is not free from any undue influence; rather it is bound in sin. So when the Bible speaks of being "free," we have to then ask, "Free from what?" And in the context of discussing the will of human beings, part of salvation is making the will of redeemed people free from the slavery of sin so that they no longer obey (live out) those sinful desires. To summarize, since what we *want* is often sinful, biblical freedom gives us the power to *not* do what we (sinfully) want. This does *not* mean that we are free to pick ourselves up by our own bootstraps, to change the nature of who we are, to redefine reality, or to live in a way contrary to the law of Christ. Thus, our "freedom" to make choices offers an explanation of evil and suffering, but further discussion is needed regarding what degree of freedom we have when we are trying to understand the nature of God's sovereignty, election, and salvation.

wishing for any to perish but for all to come to repentance.

If God were to come now, all of those who continue to hide from Him or reject Him would be lost for eternity. So one reason that suffering continues is because God is drawing more people to Himself!

Further, the Bible assures us that the suffering that God does allow us to experience has a purpose. First Peter 1:7 says,

> These [trials] have come so that your faith—of greater worth than gold, which perishes even though refined by fire—may be proved genuine and may result in praise, glory and honor when Jesus Christ is revealed.

We will get into more of what those purposes are in the next three chapters.

Next, the Bible emphatically teaches that this world is temporary (see 1 John 2:17) and that there is a promise of an eternal home void of evil, pain, and suffering—a place of peace and joy (see John 14:3; Revelation 21:4). A place where perfect relationship with God and others will be restored. A place far beyond what we could ask or imagine (Ephesians 3:20).[110]

And lastly, and perhaps most importantly, the Bible assures us that even though God asks us to endure these difficulties (see Hebrews 12:1–11), He also has powerfully demonstrated that He has not abandoned us here to deal with them alone. He has actually taken the brunt of suffering for us. The author of Hebrews writes,

---

[110] Here is one of the major limitations of the free will defense. If God can make a heaven where people do not choose to disobey Him, why can't He do it here and now? So it appears that it is not that God *cannot* make such a world; rather it is that He *has not* made this world in that way for reasons that are in accordance with bringing about His perfect will and purposes.

> For since He himself was tempted in that which He
> has suffered, He is able to come to the aide of those
> who are tempted. (2:18 NASB)

God Himself, incarnate in the person of Jesus Christ, is acquainted firsthand with the challenges of suffering that we face in this world so that He can aid us, come alongside us, and say, "Yes, this is hard, but I am here *with* you."

God did not abandon us to suffer on this earth! He entered into our suffering not only to be with us but to bring us through it. And He went a step further to suffer *for* us and take the punishment of sin in our stead. That's what we read in 1 Peter 3:18:

> For Christ died for sins once for all, the righteous for
> the unrighteous, to bring you to God. He was put
> to death in the body but made alive by the Spirit ...

Jesus Christ experienced the pinnacle of suffering in His love for us, and He did it to accomplish forgiveness and salvation and to allow Him to sympathize with us (Hebrews 4:15)!

It is here within the biblical response that we can even begin to address the emotional problem of suffering. Christian belief affirms that there is an emotional toll that suffering takes. But it doesn't say ignore it. It says acknowledge it and feel it with others—mourn with those who mourn (Romans 12:15)—just like God feels it with us. The beautiful thing about Christianity is that it not only offers potential answers to this problem to address the logical and evidential sides of the problem. It offers a person to deliver those answers—a person to walk with us as we seek those answers. A person who took the brunt of the pain for us. Thereby, it validates and offers comfort in light of the emotional problem!

In the person of Jesus Christ, can we see that it was through allowing tragic suffering and incomprehensible pain that an immeasurable, incommensurable, incomprehensible good was achieved? Through His death, we have forgiveness. Through His death, there is justice. Through His death, we are reconciled. And through His life, we have hope!

In closing, let's just summarize what we've covered. There's no logical contradiction between the existence of a good and loving God and the existence of evil or suffering. And there are arguments that can be used to make their coexistence probable, not improbable. On top of all of that, there is an emotional help within the explanations offered.

Further, we see that the Christian response to suffering affirms that evil, pain, and suffering do exist in this world. It allows for the willing choices of individuals to have real effects, which makes possible both loving and evil intentions. It acknowledges that suffering can serve a purpose. And, unique to the Christian response, it asserts that God Himself sympathizes with us—that He entered into suffering alongside us and paid the price of evil for us.

So why do we hurt? Because it has purpose. And understanding that purpose is fundamental in determining what to do about it.

4

The Physiological Problem

"The pain. The pain itself is the *problem*," I said after reasoning through our exam findings.

"Well, of course the pain is the problem!" the young intern responded with some tone of exasperation at my cryptic suggestion. "That's why she is here, because her knee hurts!"

"Yes, yes, yes. You're exactly right. Her knee does hurt, but our exam doesn't suggest that her knee is what is causing her pain. The knee isn't the problem, but the physiological process through which she is experiencing pain likely is. The pain (process) is the problem," I replied, hoping to direct the intern's clinical reasoning toward considering an alternative explanation to this young lady's pain other than traditional orthopedic pathology.

I could sense only a flicker of illumination, as the light switch had not yet fully completed the circuit. "We'll come back to this later. Let's finish our exam for now."

To help understand the purpose of pain, I think it will be helpful to know more about the science behind how we feel pain. To do that, we need to go through some of the history of how our understanding of pain physiology has evolved over the past several years.

A Brief History of Pain Theories

The scientific understanding of pain neuroscience has seen an explosion of literature in the last twenty years, leading to a call for researchers and health care providers to "reconceptualize" their view of pain.[111] There have been various theories presented— some of which are largely agreed upon and others that are more controversial—but many have profound impacts on the way pain is treated and managed. Thus, understanding pain physiology is yet another problem that is present in considering the pain and suffering in this world.

I believe that a fuller understanding of the amazing physiological processes that are in place within our bodies' biological systems provides tremendous insight into the purpose and function of pain. It shows a connection between how we hurt—physically—and how we suffer—emotionally. And because of that, it can have a profound impact on how we answer the question "Why do we hurt?" So buckle up! We are going to take a whirlwind tour of pain science!

The way people experience pain has been a mystery for centuries, and hence the theories proposed have changed over time. Only recently have health care providers and researchers had the technology available to really study what's going on within the bodies and, perhaps more importantly, minds of those who are suffering.

---

[111] G. Lorimer Moseley, "Reconceptualizing pain according to modern pain science," *Physical Therapy Reviews* 12, no. 3 (2007): 169–178.

The Cartesian Model

For the longest time, it was assumed that pain was a sensation from our body informing us of damage or injury. This was clearly suggested in the writings of Rene Descartes around the year 1664 and has become known as the Cartesian model of pain.[112] The basic idea presented by Descartes was that pain traveled through the body in tubes or channels. The example he used was that if your foot was in a fire, the skin and tissues would be burnt, creating pain in the foot, and that pain would then travel through channels in the body and make you conscious of the pain.

This theory has maintained credibility for so long because it is consistent with a lot of the pain we experience regularly. If you touch something hot, you feel pain as the skin is being damaged from the heat. When you twist your ankle playing in the backyard and some ligaments are sprained, you feel pain in the area of those ligaments.

Seems straightforward, right? It is consistent with many of the experiences we all have had—especially with acute pains from cuts, scrapes, bumps, and bruises. And it makes sense physiologically. So why question it? Well, when we really start to look at the experiences reported by individuals suffering from any injury or chronic illness, there is a wide variety of ways that people report the severity of their pain and how much it affects their life. Often there can be very similar injuries but very different experiences for different people. This begs the question "Why is there such variation in the way people experience pain?"

If pain is simply a signal of tissue injury or damage, wouldn't the same injury or amount of damage lead to the same amount of pain in all people? Also, if pain is just a sensation that is transmitted through the body, treatments that aim to block those channels should work

---

[112] Jun Chen, "History of pain theories," *Neuroscience Bulletin* 27, no. 5 (October 2011): 343–50.

with 100 percent success—which they don't. And removing the body part from the metaphorical fire should abolish the pain—which it doesn't (not always anyways).

The straightforwardness of this theory and its ability to explain many pain experiences has resulted in it being the prevailing thought for centuries. However, there are common scenarios that call this underlying assumption into question. For example, soldiers in battle can sometimes have significant injury but experience no pain. And other times, people can have incapacitating pain with no evidence of tissue injury or damage. What can explain these situations?

When we look at this from a broader perspective, there is evidence that more is going on in the pain experience than simply the transmission of a signal of damage. But the unfortunate result from applying an overly simplistic understanding of pain to these more complex situations can be a harsh or dismissive attitude by health care professionals interacting with people reporting a more severe pain experience than would be typically expected. Or the prescription could end up treating the pain through an incorrect understanding of the pain mechanism, which can lead to other problems (think opioid epidemic from chapter 1).

Let me use my own favorite sport (soccer) as an example to understand how harsh treatment can occur. Admittedly, soccer has gained a bit of a reputation over the years for some miraculous on-field recoveries from injury. If you have ever watched a soccer match, you know what I am talking about. The star forward is trying to break away from a defender and doesn't quite get the shot off that he was hoping for—and what happens? He makes a dramatic flop and roll and is writhing on the ground, screaming for about thirty seconds. Then when no penalty is called, you see him refuse medical assistance as he limps around for another fifteen seconds, only to sprint after the ball a moment later.

Our immediate response to this situation is "He's faking it!"

We conclude he's faking it because the degree to which he

displayed a pain experience does not equal the amount of damage to his body that we assume is there. Now, in this case, our assumption is almost always correct. But can you see what could happen if we repeatedly make this assumption? Someone comes to us reporting extreme pain, but we don't see any damage that can explain it. So we assume ... what? They're faking it.

Now, imagine a different situation with me. You have been having increasingly intense back pain for several months. You can't think of an injury or anything that could have caused it. But each morning you wake up, the pain is a little more severe and a little more debilitating. You are starting to get scared. *What's wrong? I am starting to have a hard time doing my job and keeping up with things around the house*, you think.

As your symptoms get worse, you decide to make an appointment at the local clinic to have an evaluation. The health care provider comes in, looks at you quizzically after reviewing some images of your back, and says, "Well, everything looks good. Just stay active. You'll be fine." Not very comforting, right?

So you go to another health care provider to get a second opinion—only to get a similar response. Then a third and fourth opinion. Finally someone asks, "What are you trying to get out of this?" Essentially, what is being asked is "Why are you faking it?" Your pain has not only been invalidated, but you have just been accused of being a liar, being manipulative, being lazy, and being a leech on society, all with one question. Ouch, right?

You know that your pain is real. All you want to do is have your life back, provide for your family, and be able to enjoy simple things like keeping up your home. But this pain is keeping you from it, and the only response you get is "Stop faking it!" Imagine how hurtful, how deflating, how infuriating this would be!

Unfortunately, this is not an uncommon scenario for a variety of pain conditions, and almost all health care specialties have been guilty of treating people with pain that is more difficult to explain in a way similar to this. Even my profession of physical therapy is not free of charge in this. But this sort of thing happens because health care has misunderstood how pain works. Pain is not a simple signal from our bodies indicating damage. It can and does do that (sometimes—even oftentimes), but that is not the only thing it does; nor is it the only factor in how it is experienced.

Passing through the Gate

A landmark shift in the way pain was understood medically occurred in the mid-1900s when two scientists, Ronald Melzack and Patrick Wall, introduced a new theory regarding pain signaling and processing. This is known as "gate control theory."[113] Essentially, this theory stated that there are connections at the spinal cord that allow other sensations and signals from within the body to transmit, magnify, dampen, or block the signal thought to trigger the pain experience.

Think about it this way: when something hurts, we often put pressure on it or maybe even get a massage to make it feel better. Why does that work? The idea is that the sense of pressure from rubbing or massaging the area would send additional signals into the spinal cord. Those pressure signals would then activate different nerves in the spinal cord (the technical term is *interneurons*), which could then block the signals causing pain coming into the spinal cord. This would then promote a process where the signals that would normally initiate a painful response would *not* get transmitted to the brain (so you wouldn't be aware of them), and, hence, less pain would be experienced.

This theory introduced a big shift in our knowledge of pain by understanding that other sensations and experiences occurring at the time of injury affect the severity of pain experienced. It is this same theory that helps to explain how many common pain treatments

---

[113] Ronald Melzack and Patrick D. Wall, "Pain mechanisms: A new theory," *Science* 150, no. 3699 (November 1965): 971–979.

like electrical stimulation, topical ointments and creams, taping, and bracing may work. They introduce another sensation that can activate interneurons, which then keep other signals that may cause pain from traveling to the brain.

This finding can lead us to ask, if physical sensations like pressure and touch affect pain, what other sensations may also affect how we feel pain? And there have been a variety of studies completed looking at this. What we find is that not only sensations coming from the body can do this, but signals occurring in the brain can too. This accounts for what we call *contextual factors* in the pain experience.[114] These are things like stress, emotions, expectations, fears, life circumstances, financial issues, family environment, cultural ideologies, and the like. What we find is that there are numerous things that can either increase or decrease the intensity of the pain experienced. In the health care field, we refer to these sorts of things as *yellow flags*[115]—psychological and social factors that are occurring outside of the medical problem that can significantly influence the treatment and experience of pain.

Consider stress as an example. Chronic and toxic stress is a common occurrence in our world today. Several reports and articles have highlighted the far-reaching effects of prolonged periods of high stress. It has been associated with numerous health conditions like irritable bowel syndrome, metabolic syndrome, cardiovascular disease, and a host of mental health issues, largely due to the

---

[114] Giacomo Rossettini, et al, "Clinical relevance of contextual factors as triggers of placebo and nocebo affects in musculoskeletal pain," *BMC Musculoskeletal Disorders* 19, no. 27 (January 2018): 1-15, https://doi.org/10.1186/s12891-018-1943-8.

[115] Michael K Nicholas, et al., "Early identification and management of psychological risk factors ("yellow flags") in patients with low back pain: A reappraisal," *Physical Therapy* 91, no. 5 (May 2011): 737–753, https://doi.org/10.2522/ptj.20100224.

imbalance of the hormone cortisol.[116] But its role in pain is becoming increasingly recognized.[117]

We all have experienced this to some degree. When we are in a new and intense situation, we become super focused, and we aren't distracted by small things. For example, if you've been working outside and trying to get your equipment in before a storm, you probably won't notice the sensation of a cut on your arm. This is the good outcome of short periods of high stress. It allows us to focus on what needs to be done.

The downside occurs if you become chronically stressed.[118] Think about a situation like this: you've been swamped with paperwork at the office, working late and going in early, and then your boss hands you another stack of paperwork to finish by noon. When you go to take the paper clip off the brick-ton of papers, you get a paper cut. This is likely to send you into a whooping and raging fit of verbal expressions of extreme pain. Why such a difference in response? The effects of stress are influencing the experience.

We experience a similar phenomenon with fear. Think about our low back pain example from earlier. When the back pain comes on without explanation, it seems to be spreading and is becoming more and more debilitating; then your mind can start running down dark alleys you've never been to before. You may start wondering

---

[116] Neil Schneiderman, et al., "Stress and Health: Psychological, behavioral, and biological determinants," *Annual Review of Clinical Psychology* 1 (2005): 607–628, https://doi.org/10.1146/annurev.clinpsy.1.102803.144141.

[117] Claire E. Lunde and Christine B. Sieberg, "Walking the tightrope: A proposed model of chronic pain and stress," *Frontiers in Neuroscience* 14, no. 270 (March 2020), https://doi.org/10.3389/fnins.2020.00270.

[118] Kara E. Hannibal and Mark D. Bishop, "Chronic stress, cortisol dysfunction, and pain: A psychoneuroendocrine rationale for stress management in pain rehabilitation," *Physical Therapy* 94, no. 12 (Deecember 2014): 1816–1825, https://doi.org/10.2522/ptj.20130597. This is an excellent article that explains the role of cortisol dysfunction and interactions with the amygdala creating programmed pain responses to stress and the systemic impacts of cortisol dysfunction on other body systems.

things like, *Did a disc slip out? Am I suffering from degenerative disc disease (whatever that is)? Will I need surgery? Oh, no! Is this cancer?* When these thoughts start happening, the pain can become a little more intense.

On the other hand, can you think of a time when you saw the doctor, and after the examination was done, he was able to confidently tell you, "Nothing is torn or broken." Or "What you are feeling is relatively common. I can help you with this." Can you recall how, after that, it seems like almost immediately the pain is better? What can account for these changes in our pain experience?

Now, admittedly, this gets more complicated (and far less humorous) when the stresses in life are more substantial, like surviving instances of trauma and abuse, or when the fear we have has to do with our own safety or the safety of our loved ones. But a similar process is occurring in these situations. The underlying physiology involves similar mechanisms.

From all of this, we can conclude that the life events surrounding a painful stimulus affect our experience of it. And so does the way we frame our experience in light of what we associate it with and what we expect. There are a few studies that have looked at simply associating a color with painful stimuli that help demonstrate this.[119] These researchers have found that people report higher levels of pain when the color red is paired with a pain-inducing sensation compared to when the same stimulus is paired with other colors, like blue for example. The reason? Red is associated with danger, alarm,

---

[119] See Moseley, "Reconceptualizing pain according to modern pain science," 169–178. Moseley's article gives a nice summary of findings from several studies. Another study was completed more recently that confirmed similar findings that simply associated different colors with painful stimuli affected the perception of pain severity across participants. See Karolina Wiercioch-Kuzianik and Przemyslaw Babel, "Color hurts. The effect of color on pain perception," *Pain Medicine* 20, no. 10 (October 2019): 1955–1962, https://doi.org/10.1093/pm/pny285.

and negativity. Thus, researchers believe that what we associate sensations with affects the way that sensation is experienced.

This is closely related to how what we anticipate about any sensation ultimately affects what we experience.[120] When a stimulus is described severely or with threatening or harmful language, people report higher levels of pain and vice versa. And this anticipation has far-reaching affects when we carry it over to what is expected not only with the pain itself but the treatment prescribed for it.

The effectiveness of "sham" treatments has led many researchers to reconsider what is often referred to as the placebo effect.[121] We often think of a placebo as something that is inert, ineffective, or does nothing. The traditional idea of a placebo treatment is a sugar pill. The patient takes a pill that is described as a powerful pain reducer or a miracle drug, but in actuality it contains no active ingredient that would have any direct effect on the symptoms. But what we repeatedly find is that even an inert sugar pill can lead to meaningful improvements in symptoms, especially when the placebo is paired with a message that the sugar pill, placebo, or sham treatment is amazingly effective.[122]

Relative to orthopedic surgeries, there have been at least seven

---

[120] Howard L. Fields, "How expectations influence pain," *Pain* 159, Supplemental 1 (September 2018): S3–S10, https://doi.org/10.1097/j.pain. 0000000000001272.

[121] Seetal Dodd, et al., "A review of the theoretical and biological understanding of the nocebo and placebo phenomena," *Clinical Therapeutics* 39, no. 3 (March 2017): 469–476, https://doi.org/10.1016/j.clinthera.2017.01.010.

[122] Several researchers have confirmed this across multiple conditions. See Lene Vase, et al., "Increased placebo analgesia over time in irritable bowel syndrome (IBS) patients is associated with desire and expectation but not endogenous opioid mechanisms," *Pain* 115, no. 3 (June 2005): 338–347, https://doi.org/10.1016/j.pain.2005.03.014; Lene Vase, et al., "The contributions of suggestion, desire, and expectation to placebo effects in irritable bowel syndrome patients. An empirical investigation," *Pain* 105, no. 1–2 (September 2003): 17–25, https://doi.org/10.1016/s0304-3959(03)00073-3; and Joel E. Bialosky, et al., "Placebo mechanisms of manual therapy: A

studies that have investigated the results of people who received sham surgery for back pain, knee pain, or shoulder pain. The summary of findings from these studies indicates that, for certain conditions, *believing* you had surgery is just as effective as receiving actual surgery![123] Isn't that interesting!

What researchers are understanding with greater clarity from these studies is that when people expect that something will be effective for their pain, the chances of them seeing improvement are much greater. And the same is true in the opposite direction. This is known as the nocebo effect—when people expect a negative result from a treatment, they are more likely to have worsened symptoms. The theme that is hopefully becoming apparent is that what we *believe* about our pain and how it is treated—how we have evaluated it—is extremely important to the ultimate outcome of how we experience that pain and its response to treatment!

At this point, I am sure some are asking, "How can my stress levels, my fears and beliefs—even colors—affect my pain? How can what I believe or anticipate about pain influence the level of pain that I have? That just sounds like psychological mumbo-jumbo and self-fulfilling prophecy type talk!"

Well, if we believe that pain is just a sensation that occurs in our body and then is felt, then yes, this sounds a little fanciful. But although some sensations—like light touch, sharp or dull, and hot or cold—behave like we would expect from the Cartesian model, these sensations are perceived by specific receptors in tissues and are experienced proportionately to a given stimulus. They are then communicated to the brain and can be mapped very clearly because they consistently activate specific brain areas that represent particular body parts. However, pain is not so simple.

sheep in wolf's clothing?" *Journal of Orthopedic & Sports Physical Therapy* 47, no.5 (May 2017): 301–304, https://doi.org/10.2519/jospt.2017.0604.

[123] Adriaan Louw, et al., "Sham surgery in orthopedics: A systematic review of the literature," *Pain Medicine* 18, no. 4 (April 2017): 736–750, https://doi.org/10.1093/pm/pnw164.

Enter the Neuromatrix

As technology continues to develop, scientists can now map the areas of the brain involved in the pain experience. When these maps are created, several areas of the brain appear to be active when pain is experienced.[124] These same areas are also very involved in stress responses, the generation of fear, short- and long-term memory, emotions and mood, decision-making, and even how we move. For example, one of the areas active during a pain response is the amygdala. This is a small, almond-shaped area in the brain that plays a crucial role in processing memory and emotions and is very involved in fear responses and addictive behaviors.

Another area of the brain that is particularly active is the anterior cingulate cortex. This plays a large role in regulating basic body functions like heart rate and blood pressure but also is involved in more cognitive functions like decision-making, evaluating costs and benefits, anticipating rewards, and the ability to focus our attention and relate with others.

The last brain area I will mention is the hypothalamus. I mention this because it is very involved in a lot of our body's automatic functions (like our endocrine system, which controls a lot of our internal hormone release—think cortisol and stress) and influences the control of body temperature, hunger, thirst, fatigue, sleep, and is critical in our bodies' responses to stress.

In recognition of these findings, there has been a huge paradigm shift in how we understand pain. Even Ron Melzack, one of the men

---

[124] G. Lorimer Moseley, "A pain neuromatrix approach to patients with chronic pain," *Manual Therapy* 8, no. 3 (August 2003): 130–140, https://doi.org/10.1016/s1356-689x(03)00051-1. See also Adriaan Louw and Emilio Puentedura, *Therapeutic Neuroscience Education: Teaching Patients About Pain*, (Minneapolis, MN: Orthopedic Physical Therapy Products, 2013), and Irene Tracey and Patrick W. Mantyh, "The cerebral signature for pain perception and its modulation," *Neuron* 55, no. 3 (August 2007): 377–391, https://doi.org/10.1016/j.neuron.2007.07.012.

who proposed the gate control theory, admits his original theory is outdated, insufficient, and needs to be updated.[125] Enter the *neuromatrix theory of pain*.[126] Whoa! It's like we just stepped into a sci-fi movie or something! It will probably feel like it at times, but I assure you these are findings based on science, not fiction.

The gate control theory revolutionized our view of pain in that it recognized the role of the spinal cord in modulating pain. The neuromatrix theory goes even further and recognizes the immense role the brain has on the pain experience. Perhaps the most notable result of this development in our understanding of the pain experience is that pain is not a sensation that arrives at the brain for us to *feel*. Rather, a variety of stimuli (those would include sensations from our body, signals from other senses like vision and taste and smell, our memories, our stress levels, our beliefs and fears, etc.) are all processed alongside one another to *produce* an experience—and here's the kicker—based on the *evaluation* of the meaning of the combined message of those signals.

What's really important to note is that because so many different brain areas are involved, and the activity in each of those brain areas is determined by a multitude of factors (e.g., genetics, previous experience, current state of health), everyone's brain activity looks a little different. Within the neuromatrix theory, this is called a *neurotag*. Essentially, this is a term used to indicate that because everyone has different genetics, past experiences, overall health status, and so on, everyone also has their own unique pain signature when it comes to the brain activity that can be measured.[127] This means that everyone's experience of pain is unique to them and is individualized, subjective, and specific.

---

[125] Ronald Melzack, "Pain and the neuromatrix in the brain," *Journal of Dental Education* 65, no. 12 (December 2001): 1378–1382.

[126] Ronald Melzack, "From the gate to the neuromatrix," *Pain,* Supplemental 6 (August 1999): S121–126, https://doi.org/10.1016/S0304-3959(99)00145-1.

[127] Tracey, "The cerebral signature for pain perception and its modulation," 377–391, https://doi.org/10.1016/j.neuron.2007.07.012.

OK, this is starting to get pretty technical, so let's see how this works. When you touch a hot stove, there are numerous receptors in your skin and underlying tissues that become activated. These receptors then send signals through the nerves that connect with them to the spinal cord (think Rene Descartes and the Cartesian model of pain). Once in the spinal cord, a number of neural connections occur—nerves from different receptors in the hand converge, nerves from the other hand connect, nerves from the wrist and arm also provide signals—and interneurons (remember our term from earlier) all interact at the spinal cord. This interaction produces a new signal, which is then relayed up the spinal cord (think gate control theory) to the brain. Once in the brain, one of the first areas that the signal arrives in is known as the thalamus. Here, *a lot* of connections occur that initiate the processing of the signal that has arrived (enter the neuromatrix!). Another area the signal arrives at is the brainstem, which aids in arousing our attention and ramping up our system in case we need to do something (like pull our hand away quickly). Some initial processing begins in the thalamus and brainstem, but numerous connections also relay the signal to other areas of the brain to be processed, essentially, simultaneously.

The signal goes to the anterior cingulate cortex to determine if this is a new pain or something that has been experienced before. This helps evaluate what the response has been to similar experiences in the past and helps determine if the response should be the same or different to help guide the selection of what action needs to occur now.

The signal also goes to the amygdala to process similar aspects of memory and brings in emotional context. This is where things like "Has this resulted in fear or anxiety in the past?" are evaluated. The hypothalamus also receives the signal (as well as signals from the other brain areas) to begin a response that releases hormones throughout the body to ready other systems (think stress response and cortisol release). Every person's unique and specific activity in these areas (and others) is what makes up their neurotag, or pain signature.

Then, each of these brain areas, being connected with one another (as well as other areas), respond to receiving the signal of heat (from touching the hot stove) by initiating a specific pattern of activity. That activity is influenced by the current level of activation in each brain area as well as the memories of previous similar instances. Once all of that is evaluated, a response is generated and reaches our conscious awareness. In this case, that response is the reflexive action of pulling our hand away and the experience of pain from a burn.

Now, this neural process appears to be true of all sensations and responses experienced during injuries or illness as well as sorrow and grief. When the sensation (physical or emotional) enters the brain, a widespread chain reaction occurs. And as this happens more and more, the neural system can become sensitive—its connections begin to activate easier and easier. The entire pattern may become hardwired together. Our neurotag can begin to get activated by things that aren't actually harmful. This is why even the memory of a painful experience can elicit pain. Or recalling the memory of a loved one who has died, even years ago, can elicit a strong emotional response. Those connections in our brain can activate our pain (physical or emotional) signature. This also explains how things like stress and fear can influence, and even stimulate, pain experiences. The brain areas involved with these make up an important part of our brain's unique pattern of activity and can enhance, or reduce, how our neurotag is activated. It is after that has happened that the experience of pain is produced.

Consider the military veteran returning from active duty and struggling with post-traumatic stress disorder after being injured by shrapnel from an explosion on his last tour of duty. The sound of a loud bang in the parking garage activates his auditory nerve, which sends signals to the brain to be processed. Those signals arrive in the thalamus and are relayed to the anterior cingulate cortex (have

I heard this before?) and the amygdala (what emotions have I had along with this stimulus?). The subconscious evaluation can be, "Yes, I have heard this before—explosion. Therefore, the appropriate emotion to experience now is fear." Stress levels rise as the pain neurotag has been activated, and he can report feeling the pain of the shrapnel—even though the injury healed months (or years) ago.

Pain can be produced by anything that activates the neurotag that makes up our own unique pain signatures.

"Given all that we know about pain neuroscience and the processing of nerve signals in the brain, can you see how the pain itself could be the issue?" I asked the resident after reviewing some of the recent pain science literature with him.

"I think so. Basically, what you are saying is that she has enough going on in her life that her entire nervous system is more easily triggered and has become wired to produce pain?" he said with an inflection that indicated this was more of a suggested answer than a concrete one.

"Exactly!" I replied emphatically. "Her unique pain neurotag—her pain signature—is being activated very easily. And when we examined her knee, it did not seem to be activated by much of our testing. But she reports so many other yellow flags—stress at home, stress at school, pain continuing beyond expected healing times, maladaptive behaviors (attempted suicide)—that we can reasonably conclude that a primary driver of her pain is coming from her body's central processing (i.e., the processing occurring in her brain), not from an *injury* in her knee."

"OK. That makes sense," came the resident's reply. "But what do we do about it then?"

"That's the question, isn't it? Do you think just giving her exercises for her knee or giving her a bigger (and better?) brace is going to help?" I didn't even wait for him to answer, as his head nodding indicated that his train of thought was right on track. "Probably not, right? But we can utilize relaxation techniques and generalized exercise for stress relief. And we can also help reintroduce activities in a scheduled manner that help to minimize how many movements and activities trigger her neurotag. But do you think that will be enough to completely get rid of her pain?"

"I guess, I don't think so," concurred the resident.

"Neither do I. Her pain is deeper than a musculoskeletal injury. We can help her, yes. But this will be a long road to recovery that will require help from multiple people."

Pain's Physiological Purpose

The more we understand about pain, the more we realize that it is something produced by the brain. It is an *output*. It is not the realization of a sensory *input*. It is a complex experience that is comprised of physical sensations, emotions, and physiological processes that are consciously and subconsciously evaluated. Pain is thought only to occur when that evaluation, in consideration of each individual person's unique circumstances, results in a specific conclusion.

Pain researcher Lorimer Moseley describes it quite well. He defines pain like this: "Pain is a multiple system output that is activated by an individual-specific pain neuromatrix ... [which] is activated whenever the brain concludes that body tissue is in danger and action is required."[128] Now, read that again with a really cool Australian accent to get the full effect! "Pain is produced to tell us we are in 'dane-ja'!"

Now, an important thing to note is that the conclusion is one of

---

[128] Moseley, "A pain neuromatrix approach to patients with chronic pain", 138.

"dane-ja," not damage. Damage can mean danger, yes. But danger does not necessarily mean damage. This is reflected in the way the International Association for the Study of Pain conceptualizes pain.[129] Their most recent definition of pain is "an unpleasant sensory and emotional experience associated with actual or potential tissue damage, or described in terms of such damage."

So pain is associated with actual or *potential* damage (or injury). This means that even if we believe that something could be harmful or injurious, we could experience pain. Or, on the flip side, if we perceive something as not harmful or damaging, we may not experience pain (even if it is, in fact, damaging!). In other words, what we *believe*, anticipate, and *perceive* about our situation and the sensations we have at the moment influence what we *feel* at that moment.

Another way to look at it is to view pain as an indicator of threat.[130] When we perceive threat, pain is often the result. That can be threat to our bodies physically or our minds emotionally.

This is all a really long and detailed way of saying that pain is like an alarm. It tells you when something is a *threat* and alerts you to it! Pain is telling you that you are in "dane-ja", and you need to do something about it, mate.

OK, OK. I bet a lot of you thinking right now, *Well, duh! I could have told you that. We didn't need the big, long lecture to arrive at that conclusion.* Which is fair. But I am going into all of this detail because I want us to see, very clearly, how many factors go into what we interpret as pain. It is really complex! But most importantly, we have seen very clearly that pain serves an extremely important *purpose.* It exists for our *protection* from a variety of things! And the

---

[129] Srinivasa N. Raja, et al., "The revised International Association for the Study of Pain definition of pain: concepts, challenges, and compromises," Pain 161, no. 9 (September 2020): 1976-1982, https://doi.org/10.1097/j.pain. 0000000000001939.

[130] Moseley, "Reconceptualising pain according to modern pain science," 171. See also Louw, *Therapeutic Neuroscience Education: Teaching Patients About Pain.*

pain experience is individualized and is unique to each of us. So, what that purpose is—what the *threat* is in our circumstance—is specific to each and every one of us. There is not a universal answer to why we hurt. But there is a unique purpose.

Let's go back to where we left off in the last chapter. I said that the challenge to the existence of a good and loving God from the reality of pain and suffering is only legitimate if that pain and suffering serves no ... what? No purpose. And what have we just thoroughly demonstrated? Pain serves a very important purpose. It is a warning signal against threat so as to avoid damage. Sometimes damage to our bodies in what we have been discussing so far, but what about damage to our souls?

What if we use our understanding of physical pain being an alarm—a warning signal of danger or threat—as an analogy to the pain and suffering we see in the world at large? We should interpret this as a glaring message that there is a threat to us in this world!

And biblically speaking, we face a very real threat in the world! Romans 8:22 states, "We know that the whole creation has been groaning as in the pains of childbirth right up to the present time."

When sin entered the world, it did not just affect the human heart. It affected everything. All of creation has fallen from what it once was and is supposed to be (see Genesis 3:14–19 and Romans 8:20). And, therefore, it presents a threat that brings actual and potential damage to our bodies and our souls.

Just look at the way the Bible describes sin. In Genesis 4:7, where God is warning Cain just before he murders his brother, He says, "Sin is crouching at your door; it desires to have you." The imagery here is that of a demon, or enemy, poised to attack and overpower its target. So, because sin entered the world and the human heart, there is a constant struggle for each of us to be overcome and overpowered by evil! And, as the verse we just read in Romans seems to indicate, it is a struggle that all of creation faces as well.

This idea is perhaps more clearly described in 1 Peter 5:8: "Be self-controlled and alert. Your enemy the devil prowls around like a roaring lion looking for someone to devour."

So, what am I saying here?

Well, if pain is an alarm system that serves as a warning against things that are either currently damaging us or that could be potentially damaging to us, then when we see pain in this world, we should interpret this as a signal that there is a threat to our well-being within this world as well, right? And this is perfectly consistent with what we read in the Bible and believe as Christians!

This world is fallen. There are threatening beings and threatening forces and threatening desires that we must be aware of, be warned of, be alert to, and resist and master.[131] The world as it is now is not what it once was, nor what it will be forever. The pain and suffering we see is a reminder that this earth has not been restored yet. It builds an "eager expectation" of the world to come (see Romans 8:19). It warns us not to get too comfortable here.

So when we see illness, natural disasters, famines, and all sorts of other tragedies, our good and right response is to recoil in disapproval because we are rightly evaluating that these things should not be so. Because they shouldn't be! These are all powerful reminders of the state of the world. It is "groaning" under the effects of sin. And we need this—especially in twenty-first-century America. How easy is it for us in and amongst all of our affluence, convenience, and luxury to feel as if life is really good? How easy is it for us to feel as if we have everything under control? How easy is it for us to forget that this world is not home and there waits for us something better? Were it not for some of the glaring evils in this world, I fear many of us (myself included) could get really attached to this world, even to the extent of preferring it over whatever else God has planned for the future.[132]

---

[131] One can just read Ephesians 6:12 for an explicit statement of the reality of evil forces and beings that we battle with.

[132] Although I do believe that this principle does help us to understand why such things as natural disasters, wars, and atrocious acts of evil that cause

Thus, pain, suffering, illness, natural disasters, famines, and wars are all powerful demonstrations that there is still something wrong in our world. We live in a dangerous place that is constantly presenting a threat to us. And as we continue to witness these things happening again and again, it affirms that our inner sense of something being wrong here is correct, and it prompts us to seek something, or someone, to save us from it.

This is starting to sound familiar, right? Look at Colossians 1:21–22:

> Once you were alienated from God and were
> enemies in your minds because of your evil behavior.
> But now he has reconciled you by Christ's physical
> body through death to present you holy in his sight,
> without blemish and free from accusation.

The pain and suffering we see in this world are perfectly consistent with the biblical teaching that the world is fallen, people are sinful (evil), and we need to be saved from our present situation. Further, it provides a wonderful bridge to introduce the truth of the Gospel and speak of the peace that faith in Christ provides!

Now I am willing to bet that someone out there is thinking, *I knew it! Here we go again. Just another fire-and-brimstone sermon on how I'm a sinner and all the pain and suffering I am facing is my fault. If I just wouldn't sin, this pain would leave me. I wouldn't have to suffer any more if I would just ask Jesus to save me from it.*

I can see how someone could interpret things that way, but that

---

human suffering occur, I do not intend to deal directly with those sorts of instances in this book. Because of that, the following chapters are written with people suffering from illness, injury, and chronic pain in mind. That being said, the principles would still apply, but how I would explain them, the examples I would give, and the emphasis I would place on certain ideas would be different if I were talking to someone who had been the victim of violent crime, for example.

is not at all what I have said. I have said that the experience of pain and suffering is consistent with the biblical teaching of sin and a fallen world—in *principle*. I have put forth a position that allows us to see that pain can serve a *purpose*. I am saying that because sin has entered the world, pain and suffering can exist to warn us of that reality in order to prompt us to action. One action may be to repent of our own sin. Another action may be to relieve the suffering we see around us. But I have said nothing about why individual people suffer. That is the personal problem of pain—why is God allowing *me* to go through hurts, sorrows, pains, and suffering?

Now, one of the reasons that God allows each of us to experience pain and suffering is to make us aware of our own sin, yes. But the wonderful thing about Christianity is that its teachings offer multiple answers to the question of why we suffer individually. So the personal problem of pain is discerning which of those options applies to us in our unique situation.

Trying to wrestle with that question is what we will discuss next.

5

The Personal Problem in Principle

"Why is this happening to me?" she asked. I could see her trying to hold back tears as we were finishing up one of her exercises.

I had been working with Linda[133] for several months now. She had been through a lot—to put it lightly. She had had over a dozen surgeries at some point in the last eight years due to injuries sustained in a car accident. The initial intention was just to have two, but due to postsurgical complications, one operation had to be revised, and after the other planned surgery, she acquired an infection, which resulted in multiple "wash out" procedures. Now she was seeing me for arm pain and weakness. Her other doctors and I were pretty confident this was coming from a nerve issue in her neck. This led her to pursue an injection, which not only didn't help her arm pain but now gave her neck pain!

I wasn't entirely sure how to answer her. She was working hard and doing everything we, on her medical team, had asked her to do. I was using every clinical tool I could think of—modifying her exercises, utilizing therapeutic modalities, asking her to carefully monitor her responses to treatments—and we were only making

---

[133] Linda is not her real name, but this is a paraphrase representative of interactions I have had with patients.

marginal improvements at best! From a health care perspective, I couldn't really provide her a great answer as to why things weren't getting better.

But before I was able to begin my attempt at a gentle response of how "Pain is very complex. Nerves are very slow to heal, but they can. Nerves can alter their sensitivity to different sensations pretty rapidly, so there is still hope. We just have to ...," she filled the silence by continuing her question. And continuing it in a way that revealed that she didn't care about the medical answer. She wasn't as concerned with *how* she was hurting physiologically. She wanted to know *why* she was hurting teleologically.

"I have prayed for healing. I have asked God to increase my faith. I read and claim scripture over my situation. But it seems like things just keep getting worse! Why is God letting this happen to me?"

Linda was getting right to the heart of the issue. Her pain was not only a challenge for her physically; it posed a problem to her faith and thereby her relationship with, and understanding of, God. Her pain revealed a conflict between what her present situation was and what she believed about God and His promises to her. This is why the problem(s) of pain so often have theological undertones.

What purpose does pain serve in Linda's life, in your life, and in my life? It's easy to philosophize and theorize and speak abstractly about pain and suffering when all is well. But what about when we are in the heat of it? What about when the pressure is on and all around us seems to be falling apart and God's presence seems so far away? How do we answer this question then?

This is really the question that we all want answered. And since it is asked with a theological implication, we need to answer it from a theological perspective. All of the analogies we can draw from human experience (i.e., metaphors from pain neuroscience, arguments from morality and moral reasoning, deferring to free will and human choice) are all ways that can help in understanding that pain *can* serve a purpose. But to understand *what* that purpose is, if we believe that it is God's purpose that is being served, we have to turn our attention to God Himself and ask Him.

To determine the why behind pain and suffering, we have to look at what God has said about this issue in the Bible.[134] So we are going to switch gears in this chapter and carefully look at a place in the Bible that explicitly addresses this issue. The book of first Peter. This is a letter written to suffering Christians, and right away in the first chapter, Peter provides us a few reasons for suffering.[135]

The passage reads like this:

> Though now for a little while you may have had to suffer grief in all kinds of trials. These have come so that your faith—of greater worth than gold, which perishes even though refined by fire—may be proved genuine and may result in praise, glory, and honor when Jesus Christ is revealed. Though you have not seen him, you love him; and even though you do not see him now, you believe in him and are filled with an inexpressible and glorious joy, for you are receiving the goal of your faith, the salvation of your souls. (1 Peter 1:6–9)

We are going to break this passage down in order to identify

---

[134] At this point, I am assuming a primarily Christian audience, where we believe that the Bible is God's Word to us. For a brief treatment on establishing the Bible as the Word of God, see *When Skeptics Ask*, edited by Norman L. Geisler and Ronald M. Brooks (Grand Rapids, MI: Baker Books, 2013). Or for a more thorough treatment of this topic, see *Taking God At His Word* by Kevin DeYoung (Wheaton, IL: Crossway, 2014).

[135] See the introduction of John MacArthur's *New Testament Commentary Series: 1 Peter* (Chicago, IL: Moody Publishers, 2004). Or, Chuck Swindoll, *New Testament Insights. 1 Peter*, (Grand Rapids, MI: Zondervan, 2010).

three broad principles regarding the reasons for personal suffering. These then will set the stage for us as we dive into discussing each of these in more detail in the next chapter.

Principle #1

First of all, let's look at verse 6: "though now for a little while you may have had to suffer grief in all kinds of trials."

Right away, Peter is acknowledging that individuals may have to *suffer* and that suffering may take on various forms. It may present itself in *"all kinds* of trials." So we are cued in here that Peter is discussing a wide variety and numerous forms of suffering. Therefore, the following statements can be interpreted as laying down broad principles.

Then in verse 7, he moves into his explanation. We read, "These have come *so that* ..." The English phrase here "so that" is the translation of the Greek word *hina*.[136] This word is used to join two phrases in a way denoting *purpose*. Because of that, we can not only interpret this word as "so that" like we read in most translations, but it can also be understood as "for the purpose that" or "in order that."

This word tells us that what follows is providing the intent of, purpose for, and the desired result from when we "suffer grief in all kinds of trials" that the apostle Peter just mentioned. So at this point, we should really pay attention to what he is about to say!

Continuing to read from verse 7 then: "These have come *so that* your faith ... may be proved genuine" (emphasis mine).

Here we have principle one: God allows suffering in our lives to prove our faith genuine.

I know someone reading this is thinking to themselves, *Wait, what? I'm here, aren't I? I've been reading this guy's monologue go on for pages and pages. And I go to church on Sunday mornings ... the*

---

[136] "HELPS Word-studies", Discovery Bible., accessed through BibleHub. com at https://biblehub.com/greek/2443.htm

majority of the time. I say my prayers. I know of the work of Jesus. I'm
set, right? My faith is obviously genuine!

I know. I hear you. We often like to draw confidence from all
those Christian activities that we do. But this verse should cause a
very sobering pause for all of us. The first principle Peter identifies is
that our faith may need proving and testing. And this is not foreign
to the New Testament; nor is it an isolated teaching. James says the
same thing in verses 2 to 4 of the first chapter in his epistle:

> Consider it pure joy, my brothers whenever you
> face trials of many kinds, because you know that
> *the testing of your faith* develops perseverance.
> Perseverance must finish its work so that you may
> be mature and complete, not lacking anything
> (emphasis mine).

Even Abraham, the patriarch of faith, needed to have his faith
tested. Remember the story of God asking him to sacrifice his son,
Isaac (see Genesis 22:1)?[137]

But we see in the passage in James that testing produces
perseverance. The apostle Paul expands on the idea of developing
perseverance in Romans 5. He says,

> But we rejoice in our sufferings, because we know
> that suffering produces perseverance; perseverance,
> character; and character, hope. And hope does not
> disappoint us, because God has poured out his love
> into our hearts by the Holy Spirit, whom he has
> given us. (v. 3–5)

---

[137] One can only imagine the emotional difficulty of such a test. But Hebrews
11:17–19 informs us that Abraham's faith was not only in the rightness of
obeying God but also in God's power to raise his son from the dead. This story
is certainly providing us an example of faith to follow but more importantly
is foreshadowing the sacrifice and resurrection of Christ!

So Paul adds to perseverance the idea of building character (which we will discuss more later) and hope. What's more is that hope is found in the *love* of God.

This helps us to see how persevering through trials and seeing them as tests prove our faith. And that's because the genuineness of our faith is found in a love of God for God Himself. We love Him for *who* He is and the love He has shown us on the cross. This is precisely what we read in "the other" John 3:16: "This is how we know what love is: Jesus Christ laid down his life for us" (1 John 3:16).

The passage goes on to say.

> And we ought to lay down our lives for our brothers. If anyone has material possessions and sees his brother in need but has no pity on him, how can the love of God be in him? Dear children, let us not love with words or tongue but with actions and in truth. This then is how we know that we belong to the truth. (1 John 3:16–19)

So knowing the love of God and having that love affect how we live and act is one way that our faith is tested or proven. It helps us to "know that we belong to the truth." But the love that we show comes from a love *of* God, and a knowledge of the love He has shown us through His Son, not for the blessings He can give us. Right? That's the whole context of the book of Job.[138]

Remember what Satan's accusation of Job's righteousness was? Turning to the book of Job in chapter 1, we read,

> "Does Job fear God for nothing?" Satan replied. "Have you not put a hedge around him and his household and everything he has? You have blessed

---

[138] Keller, *Walking with God through Pain and Suffering*, see chapters 10 and 14.

the work of his hands, so that his flocks and herds are spread through the land. But stretch out your hand and strike everything he has, and he will surely curse you to your face." (v. 9–11)

What Satan is saying here is that Job doesn't actually "fear" (otherwise translated revere or stand in awe of) God for who He is, but he accuses Job's faithfulness to be out of a selfish desire for the good things that God has done for him. So, principle one is saying, when all is stripped away—when we have nothing left on this earth, when we face pain and suffering—can we still say, "God, I know You are good. I know what You have done for me. I know that You love me. I know the joys of knowing You even though for a little while I may have to suffer to make sure that I love You and not simply the blessings You give me"?

To summarize principle one: suffering proves our faith in, and love for, God is genuine by refocusing our hearts on Him and not the blessings He gives us. It can warn us of the *threat*[139] of a wayward and idolatrous heart.

Principle #2

The second principle[140] is closely related to the first and is found in verse 9 of our passage in 1 Peter: "for you are receiving the goal of your faith, the salvation of your souls."

---

[139] Remember the overarching principle of pain we learned in the last chapter; pain is experienced when there is an evaluation of actual or potential damage—or *threat*.

[140] I have jumped ahead to verse 9 to place the principles in an order that seems to me to build upon their importance and to end with the final paramount principle of sharing the Gospel. Admittedly, I have taken some license in placing the principles in an order not found in the text itself. I trust that this does not do injustice to the text or diminish the truth of the passage or alter what the passage itself is teaching in any way.

What we see stated here is that the goal of our faith is our salvation. And from this being a continued thought following Peter's use of "so that," it is reasonable to conclude that one of the reasons God allows suffering is to work toward our salvation.

The question on your mind right now is probably something like "How does this work? Isn't salvation through faith alone? Somebody get this guy a Bible and have him read Ephesians 2:8–9!"

Right, right. Fair objection. If we read through this quickly or superficially, we may see this as a point of conflict between two teachings in the Bible. In Ephesians, we read,

> For by grace you have been saved through faith; and this is not of yourselves, it is the gift of God; not a result of works, so that no one may boast. (2:8–9 NASB)

Whereas, here in 1 Peter we read:

> Even though now for a little while, if necessary, you have been distressed by various trials, so that the proof of your faith, being more precious than gold which perishes though tested by fire, may be found to result in praise, glory, and honor at the revelation of Jesus Christ ... obtaining as the outcome of your faith, the salvation of your souls. (1:6–7, 9 NASB)

So in Ephesians, we read that we are saved by faith apart from works, but in 1 Peter, it seems that our salvation is obtained after we have proven our faith. Does this mean that some kind of trial must be passed? Does this mean that suffering is a necessary component of our faith that must be demonstrated?

Because of this *apparent* conflict, we should proceed with careful attention to detail. First of all, let it be absolutely clear that we are saved by faith in the atoning work of Jesus Christ on the cross (see

Mark 16:16; John 3:16; Acts 16:31; Romans 10:9; Ephesians 1:7; Colossians 1:14; 1 Timothy 1:15; 2 Timothy 2:11). Jesus Christ is the ultimate source of our salvation and nothing else (see Galatians 1:6–9). However, sometimes that simple faith *may* need to be tested (e.g., Exodus 20:20; Deuteronomy 8:2).

Our passage in 1 Peter states, "if necessary." This indicates that the proving of faith through "various trials" is not a requirement for all but may be needed for some "if necessary." Peter even seems to be emphasizing the role of faith in our ability to endure trials by reminding us of the hope we have in Christ Jesus and the faith we can have in God's power to bring about our salvation. He introduces this passage by saying,

> Praise be to the God and Father of our Lord Jesus Christ! In his great mercy he has given us new birth into a living hope through the resurrection of Jesus Christ from the dead, and into an inheritance that can never perish, spoil or fade—kept in heaven for you, who through faith are shielded by God's power until the coming of the salvation that is ready to be revealed in the last time. (1 Peter 1:3–5)

So, what is Peter referring to with regards to our salvation being linked to our trials? Let me point out here that salvation is a very theologically rich concept that includes various ideas and principles. It is so rich that it has been given its own branch of study: soteriology! It is in the richness and depth of this concept that provides a fuller understanding of this passage.

Theologians have understood salvation to include several aspects. If we list them out, our salvation includes (soteriologically) things like our regeneration, our conversion, our redemption, our justification, our adoption, our sanctification, our reconciliation, and our glorification.[141] Each of these is a full discussion in and of itself, but a quick (and hopefully not cursory) definition of these could be as follows.

Regeneration is the process through which the Holy Spirit imparts spiritual life to us. It is the *start* of making us into a "new creation" and us walking in "new life" (see John 1:13 and 3:8; 2 Corinthians 5:17).[142] Conversion is our conscious response to God's call and to the knowledge of Christ and His work (see Mark 1:15; Romans 10:8–17).[143] Redemption is the act of buying us back from the power of sin through the blood of Christ (see Mark 10:45).[144] Adoption is God welcoming us into His family as sons and daughters (see Ephesians 1:5).

Justification is the legal act[145] of God whereby we are freed from the charges of sin because Christ's blood paid the penalty for us (see Romans 5:9; 2 Corinthians 5:21; Ephesians 1:7; Hebrews 9:14; 1 John 2:2).[146] Therefore, we are seen as righteous in His sight. This is closely related to redemption (see Romans 3:20–28). Sanctification is the process of refining us as a "new creation" (see 2 Corinthians 5:17), setting us apart from the world and to Himself (see 1 Corinthians 1:2; Hebrews 10:14), and conforming us to the pattern of living displayed by Christ (see Romans 8:29; 2 Corinthians 3:18), making

---

[141] See John MacArthur and Richard Mayhue, *Biblical Doctrine: A Systematic Summary of Bible Truth* (Wheaton, IL: Crossway, 2017) and Wayne Grudem's *Systematic Theology*.

[142] Wayne Grudem, "Regeneration," *Systematic Theology*, 699. And, MacArthur & Mayhue, "The Application of Redemption," *Biblical Doctrine*, 580

[143] MacArthur and Mayhue, "The Application of Redemption," *Biblical Doctrine*, 590 and Grudem, "Conversion (Faith and Repentance)," *Systematic Theology*, 709.

[144] Stan Norman, "Redeem, Redemption, Redeemer," *Holman Illustrated Bible Dictionary*, ed. Chad Brand (Nashville, TN: B&H Publishing, 2015), 1339.

[145] Grudem, "Justification (Right legal standing before God)," *Systematic Theology*, 723.

[146] MacArthur and Mayhue, "The Application of Redemption, *Biblical Doctrine*, 609

us "mature and complete" (see James 1:4).[147] Reconciliation is the restoration of the relationship that God intended to have with us (see 2 Corinthians 5:18–19). And glorification is the final completion of all of this (see Romans 8:17; 1 Corinthians 15:51–52).[148] So again, what part of our salvation is being referred to in 1 Peter 1:9?[149]

From analyzing the verse itself, we are given a few clues. One is that salvation is referred to as the "goal" or "outcome" of our faith. The Greek word being translated here is *telos,* which is from a root meaning to "reach an end."[150] The idea is one of consummation or arriving at the end goal or purpose and seeing *all* of the intended results. So, to some extent, the entire range of meanings and concepts associated with salvation are in mind. This makes sense because a tested and proven faith will surely result in the outcome that God promises to give by grace through faith (cf. Ephesians 2:8–9). But we get another clue from the verb tense just prior to this.

The verse says, "you *are* receiving." Both the English and the Greek are in the *present* tense. So the reason for suffering, as it pertains to our salvation, has to do with something that is happening *now*. Regeneration, conversion, redemption, justification, and adoption have all occurred—*past* tense. The Spirit has stirred our hearts (regeneration), and we have responded (conversion) to that to some extent (perhaps that is why you are reading this book and familiar with this passage). Redemption and justification occurred on the cross over two thousand years ago. And adoption occurred

---

[147] MacArthur and Mayhue, "The Application of Redemption," *Biblical Doctrine,* 632

[148] Grudem, "Glorification (Receiving a resurrection body)," *Systematic Theology,* 829

[149] Although we can make distinctions in these different terms, we should be careful not to view them as mutually exclusive from one another. They work together and overlap in many ways; they are all parts, or aspects, of the overarching process of our salvation.

[150] HELPS Word-studies, Discovery Bible, Bible Hub, accessed April 28, 2020, https://biblehub.com/greek/5056.htm.

at the moment the Holy Spirit took dwelling within us to begin His work (see Romans 8:15). Those are all done deals. So we see here components of the saving grace of God through our faith mentioned in Ephesians 2:8–9, "we are saved by faith." Notice the perfect tense of the verb *saved*.[151] The perfect tense indicates completed action with present results. The saving work of Christ happened in the *past* and is *now* working for us through God's *saving* grace.

Then reconciliation and glorification are components that come along with the completion of salvation—*future* tense. Here on this earth, we "know in part" (1 Corinthians 13:9 and 12), and only later will we "know fully" and "be fully known" (1 Corinthians 13:12). The phrases to "know in part" and to "know fully" are contrasting two Greek words for *knowing*. The first is *gnosis,* and the second is *epignosis*. What's important to note here is that *epignosis* intensifies the meaning of knowing through direct personal experience or relationship. So the idea of "knowing and being fully known" alludes to a restored relationship—reconciliation. The apostle John makes a clear statement as to when this personal knowledge will be made complete. In 1 John 3:2, we read, "But we know that *when he [Jesus] appears*, we shall be like him, for we shall see him as he is" (emphasis mine).

So our complete knowledge of God will be given upon Christ's return, and then reconciliation will be complete.[152] Therefore, this aspect of our salvation will reach its consummation in the future.

Likewise, glorification is also alluded to in this same verse in 1

---

[151] See Greek translation and grammatical construction of the verse at Bible Hub, accessed March 20, 2021, https://biblehub.com/text/ephesians/2-8.htm.

[152] Now there is certainly an element of this that occurs immediately in the sense that we are made right with God—that is proclaimed in right standing or declared righteous, and we have been washed and cleansed from our sin (see Titus 3:5). However, that is more closely in line with the theological concept of justification. As it stands, we are yet sinful, and therefore, to some degree, we remain separated from God while on this earth. Therefore, complete and perfect reconciliation is something that is in the future.

John. It says, "We *shall be* like him." The future tense of the verb[153] indicates that this is something that is yet to occur. It is something that will happen in the future. Philippians 3:21 also teaches this. We read, "[The Lord Jesus Christ] who, by the power that enables him to bring everything under his control, *will* transform our lowly bodies so that they *will be* like his glorious body" (emphasis mine). This verse makes clear that our complete transformation into a restored and "glorious" body (that is our *glorification* and the final completion of salvation) is something that is yet to happen. It is in the future, but we are assured that Christ will bring it to completion (see Philippians 1:6).

Thus, our complete reconciliation and glorification are aspects of our salvation that are yet to occur. They are in the future. Returning then to our passage in 1 Peter, the aspect of salvation that is most likely in the mind of the apostle Peter in verse 9 is our sanctification—*present* tense (see Hebrews 10:14).[154]

To help see this, let's look at the passage alongside what we read in chapter 4 of this epistle. Verses 1–2 read as follows:

---

[153] See Greek translation and grammatical construction of the verse at Bible Hub, accessed March 12, 2021, https://biblehub.com/text/1_john/3-2.htm.

[154] In Hebrews 10:14, we read, "For by a single offering he has perfected for all time those who *are being sanctified*" (ESV; emphasis mine). The italicized phrase is present tense participle modifying "who." The who being those people God has saved through the "one sacrifice" (Hebrews 10:12) or "single offering." This verse indicates that the process of sanctification is an ongoing process that occurs during the life of a believer in Christ. Granted, there are some verses that utilize terminology for sanctification in past tense (e.g., Acts 20:32 and 26:18; 1 Corinthians 1:2). This has been referred to as "initial, positional, or definitive sanctification" (MacArthur and Mayhue, *Bible Doctrine*, 632). However, we can use a similar reasoning as above where this component of "being made holy" or "being sanctified" is closely in line with concepts like justification and regeneration (see 1 Corinthians 6:11), which occurred immediately and are therefore in the past. As always, we have to be careful with making the distinctions between these terms too strict, as they are all descriptions of our salvation and are indissolubly linked.

> Therefore, since Christ suffered in his body, arm
> yourselves also with the same attitude, because he
> who has suffered in his body is done with sin. As a
> result, he does not live the rest of his earthly life for
> evil human desires, but rather for the will of God.
> (1 Peter 4:1–2)

So we see that the "goal of our faith" is the "salvation of our
souls" (1:9), which is worked out through the transformation of
our "evil human desires" over to the desires of God's will (4:2),
which is essentially the work of sanctification. And, during this
transformation, it is suffering that purifies us so that we can be
"done with sin" (4:1).[155]

Now, notice what I am *not* saying. I did *not* say because you have
sinned in this way or that way, you are now suffering. No. That is
not necessarily how this works. It can work that way. Suffering *may*
be a consequence of sin that is meant to bring about repentance and
aid in the work of sanctification. Either way though, I *am* saying
because you are *sinful*, your soul needs salvaging. It needs salvation.
And the process by which that is achieved is through refinement,
through purification, through discipline, through *sanctification* done
by a loving Father.

Remember what we read in Hebrews 12 verses 10 and 11:

---

[155] This should not be taken so far as to mean perfectionism where we never
sin again. The verb *is done with* is in the perfect tense, which often refers to a
past action leading to present consequence. This indicates that past suffering
(completed action) is one way to purify us from some particular sin or sins
(present consequence), not necessarily all sin in general. It is clear from 1 John
1:8 that we do not achieve perfection on this earth, but rather we strive as the
apostle Paul did when he says, "Not that I have already obtained it all or have
already become perfect, but I press on so that I may lay hold of that for which
also I was laid hold of by Christ Jesus" (Philippians 3:12 NASB).

> But God disciplines us for our good, that we may share in his holiness. No discipline seems pleasant at the time, but painful. Later on, however, it produces a harvest of righteousness and peace for those who have been trained by it.

Now, sometimes this discipline can be a form of suffering that is a result of specific sins leading to specific consequences, but not always or universally. Suffering works toward our sanctification by not only revealing the consequences of our actual sin but also warning us of the dangers of potential sin and to bring us to repentance (remember the goal of this process is to "discipline us *for our good*"), and it can also grow our perseverance, character, humility, and sympathy[156] "that we may share in His [God's] holiness" (v. 10).

At this point, we have to substantiate each of these things. So let's spend a little time looking at the biblical evidence for each of these reasons for pain and suffering that can aid in our sanctification.

First, does God allow us to suffer as a consequence of sin? The short answer is yes. The longer answer is yes but not always. And the more complete answer will come in the next chapter when we consider the story of David. But we need only to look at the first human beings to see that this is true to some extent. What happened in the Garden of Eden? Adam and Eve disobeyed God, and God distributed consequences. God said to Adam,

> Cursed is the ground *because of you*; through painful toil you will eat of it all the days of your life. It will produce thorns and thistles for you, and you will eat the plants of the field. By the sweat of your brow you will eat your food until you return to the

---

[156] This is not meant to be an exhaustive list, as there are likely more attributes that we could list that can result from enduring trials and suffering. However, these qualities are listed because of the clear biblical support for them, which is discussed in the following paragraphs.

ground, since from it you were taken; for dust you are and to dust you will return. (Genesis 3:17–19; emphasis mine)

To Eve, He said,

I will greatly increase your pains in childbearing; with pain you will give birth to children. Your desire will be for your husband, and he will rule over you. (Genesis 3:16)

And to the serpent, He said,

Because you have done this, cursed are you above all the livestock and all the wild animals! You will crawl on your belly and you will eat dust all the days of your life. And I will put enmity between you and the woman, and between your offspring and hers; he will crush your head, and you will strike his heel. (Genesis 3:14–15; emphasis mine)

To conclude the story of the Fall, we read of one final consequence that God dealt out. Adam and Eve were banished from the garden (Genesis 3:23).

In the account of the Fall, we see that every individual involved in the story received some kind of consequence for their disobedience—their sin. It's important to note though that God still showed tremendous mercy in that He did not immediately end their lives[157] (remember that's what He said was the consequence for eating the fruit of the tree in Genesis 2:17, and we know that "the wages of

---

[157] Certainly, a form of spiritual death occurred immediately, and the result of Adam's sin is believed to be what instituted physical death over the course of our earthly lives. But it would have been within God's justice to end their lives immediately, which He did not do and, in that sense, He was surely merciful.

sin is death" from Romans 6:23). He even clothed them by making garments for them (Genesis 3:21). So was there consequence and punishment for sin? Yes. Were Adam and Eve exempted from God's mercy and grace and salvation? No. I believe the same can be true of us. We *may* experience consequences of our individual sin. Thus, it is important that we "confess [our] sins to one another, and pray for one another so that [we] may be healed"[158] (James 5:16 NASB).[159]

Having said that, let us remember that temporal suffering (even if a result of our own personal sin) is meant to bring us to repentance and that we ought to view our "momentary affliction" in light of an "eternal weight of glory"! (2 Corinthians 4:17). So we are not talking about an eternal consequence but a "light and momentary affliction"—a rebuke—to get us back on track. Like the discipline of a loving father.

No matter if our sin brings direct consequences in the form of suffering or not, being aware of our sin should bring a form of suffering—like that of sorrow and mourning (see 2 Corinthians

---

[158] I cite this verse not to imply that confession and prayer will bring about physical healing. There is debate among theologians as to how to interpret this verse regarding what sort of healing is being referred to here. Rather, I cite this verse to reinforce the fact that our confession of sin is closely linked with making us well—in a spiritual sense for sure, and potentially even in a physical sense.

[159] To ensure clarity, my point here is only to acknowledge that some of the suffering we experience during our lives can be the result of our personal and individual sin. I think we can all think of times that we have experienced this. Just think of the anguish we feel through guilt when we realize that we have wronged someone, or we did something foolish while trying to show off our athletic prowess and turned an ankle. So our own sin is one reason for pain and suffering. I am not intending to say that physical pain or illness is necessarily the result of a person's individual sin, although I don't think we can say that is impossible. Consider Proverbs 14:30 that says, "Envy rots the bones," or Psalm 38:3 when David says, "My bones have no soundness because of my sin." So I think it is possible that physical ailments are the result of individual sin; however, arriving at that conclusion should be done with much prayer and caution.

7:10). It is this form of suffering that brings about repentance and humility. We also see this described in the Beatitudes.

> Blessed are the poor in spirit,
> for theirs is the kingdom of heaven.
> Blessed are those who mourn,
> for they will be comforted.
> Blessed are the meek,
> for they will inherit the earth.
> Blessed are those who hunger and thirst for righteousness,
> for they will be filled.
> Blessed are the merciful,
> for they will be shown mercy.
> Blessed are the pure in heart,
> for they will see God.
> Blessed are the peacemakers,
> for they will be called sons of God.
> Blessed are those who are persecuted because of righteousness,
> for theirs is the kingdom of heaven. (Matthew 5:3–10)

Poorness in spirit (acknowledgement of our sin and shortcomings) is followed by mourning (emotional and even physical discomfort—a form of pain and suffering), is followed by meekness, is followed by a hunger and thirst for righteousness, is followed by mercy, is followed by purity of heart, is followed by peace, is followed by persecution (which usually entails some degree of pain and suffering).

So a certain amount of the pain and suffering we experience in this world is a result of our own sin. Yes. However, it is not always that way, nor is all of the pain and suffering we witness and experience because of that. We should not immediately conclude that ours (or someone else's!) suffering is due to personal sin. Jesus

Himself readily provides an example where suffering (in the form of blindness) was not a result of that man's sin or anyone else's (see John 9:2–3).[160] We have been provided several other potential reasons for suffering, so those reasons should be considered as well.

Some of the suffering we experience may also be to warn us of potential sin. Romans 15:4 (NASB) tells us, "For whatever was written in earlier times was written for our instruction."

So when we see the suffering of David for his own sin, when we see the stories of God's judgment coming down on nations, cities, and peoples for their sins, when we realize the suffering and pain those instances brought about and caused, it can warn us of the danger of continuing in our own sin or embarking down similar paths.

Here we can allow the Word of God to act as a search light into our souls, if you will. Like we read in Hebrews,

> For the word of God is living and active. Sharper than any double-edged sword, it penetrates even to dividing soul and spirit, joints and marrow; it judges the thoughts and attitudes of the heart. Nothing in all creation is hidden from God's sight. Everything is uncovered and laid bare before the eyes of him to whom we must give an account. (4:12–13)

God's Word and the stories of the consequences of sin in the Bible can enlighten our hearts and minds to prompt us to avoid temptation or stumbling into sin. And I think God can use the suffering that is witnessed in our own lives to do the same. Think

---

[160] This passage could warrant an entire discussion in and of itself from which I will defer for the moment. But it is important to note that here Jesus says the reason this man was blind was so that the work of God may be displayed. In other words, so that God may be glorified. So we do well to remember that God can use things that are challenging from our perspective *now* to bring about His glory in the *future*.

about the suffering brought about by correcting one another. If we have to confront sin in the life of a close friend or relative, this brings a lot of emotional turmoil (suffering). And sometimes it can lead to the loss of relationships. But this is meant to restore your fellow Christian (see Matthew 18:15) and to bring about repentance (see 1 Corinthians 5:5). This sort of thing is explicitly said to serve as a warning to others in 1 Timothy 5:20. So learning of, witnessing, and even experiencing some forms of pain and suffering can serve as a warning to us to watch our own lives (see Galatians 6:1).

Next, suffering can grow our perseverance and character. This is exactly what we read in Romans 5:

> But we also rejoice in our sufferings, because we know
> that suffering produces perseverance; perseverance,
> character, and character, hope. (v. 3–4)

The idea of perseverance is closely related to our first principle (testing and proving our faith), yet it also has some role in our sanctification as well (principle two). In Hebrews 10:35, we are told that we "need to persevere." I think part of this is to indicate to us that we must draw on Christ as the source of strength in order to persevere through trials. That's what is indicated in Hebrews 12:2–3 when we are instructed to "look to Jesus" and "consider him who endured (persevered)." In that way, when we suffer, we can grow in the "fellowship of his [Jesus's] sufferings" (Philippians 3:10) and through that be made more like Him, which is sanctification.

Further, enduring pain and suffering can also serve as a future assurance in the event of more difficult trials to come. The author of Hebrews encourages his readers,

> Remember those earlier days after you had received
> the light, when you stood your ground in a great
> contest in the face of suffering. (Hebrews 10:32)

What we see here is instruction to allow the endurance of previous suffering help encourage and aid in persevering through present suffering. So the pain you are experiencing now may be serving as a necessary period of training for a greater trial to come. It increases our ability to persevere!

All of this perseverance also serves the purpose of growing us in our character. Remember it is character that follows perseverance in Romans 5:3. To help see this a little more clearly, look at how the apostle Peter describes the work we are to do in response to our faith:

> Make every effort to add to your faith goodness; and to goodness, knowledge; and to knowledge, self-control; and to self-control, perseverance; and to perseverance, godliness; and to godliness, brotherly kindness; and to brotherly kindness, love. (2 Peter 1:5–7)

Here we see that perseverance is closely related to self-control, godliness, brotherly kindness, and love. These are all aspects of our character that are produced along with perseverance through trials. Notice the similarity here to the qualities listed as the fruit of the Spirit in Galatians 5:

> But the fruit of the Spirit is *love*, joy, peace, patience, *kindness*, *goodness*, faithfulness, gentleness, *self-control*; against such things there is no law. (v. 22–23 NASB; emphasis mine)

Another reason that God can allow suffering in our lives is to develop our ability to persevere and to grow our character in such a way that the fruit of His Spirit is more evident in our lives. Again, this is part of the process of sanctification.

Yet another element of our character that may be developed through suffering and trials is humility. We see this in the apostle

Paul where he admits to a "thorn in the flesh." He describes this in his second letter to the Corinthians:

> To keep me from becoming conceited because of these surpassingly great revelations, there was given me a thorn in my flesh, a messenger of Satan, to torment me. (12:7)

Now, what this thorn was is a mystery, but Paul describes this as something that "tormented" him. And he tells us explicitly that this was given him "to keep him from becoming conceited." In other words, Paul's thorn in the flesh was meant to keep him humble.

Paul goes on to tell us,

> Three times I pleaded with the Lord to take it away from me. But he said to me, "My grace is sufficient for you, for my power is made perfect in weakness." Therefore I will boast all the more gladly about my weaknesses, so that Christ's power may rest on me. That is why, for Christ's sake, I delight in weakness, in insults, in hardships, in persecutions, in difficulties. For when I am weak, then I am strong. (v. 8–10)

What we see here is that this "torment," or suffering, kept Paul humble so that he could boast of Christ's power. Paul's thorn kept his ego in check so that he could realize the sufficiency of God's grace and experience the power of God to sustain him through insults, hardships, persecutions, and difficulties (otherwise known as trials and suffering).

Lastly, suffering can serve the purpose of building compassion and sympathy. In Hebrews 4:15–16, we read,

> For we do not have a high priest who is unable to sympathize with our weaknesses, but we have one who has been tempted in every way, just as we are—yet was without sin. Let us then approach the throne of grace with confidence, so that we may receive mercy and find grace to help us in our time of need.

This passage is describing Jesus as the "Great High Priest," and we see that Jesus willingly subjected Himself to weakness and temptation. Then Hebrews 2:18 tells us that He experienced suffering as well. And He did all of this so that He can *sympathize* with us. But this sympathy is not just to feel with us; it is to provide us access to his *mercy* and *grace* to *help* us!

So when we suffer and experience this grace and mercy, it allows us to be able to provide a similar help by directing others to the ultimate source of grace when they are going through trials or experiencing suffering.

Consider what we read in 2 Corinthians 1:3–7:

> Praise be to the God and Father of our Lord Jesus Christ, the Father of compassion and the God of all comfort, who comforts us in all our troubles, *so that we can comfort those in any trouble with the comfort we ourselves have received from God*. For just as the sufferings of Christ flow over into our lives, so also through Christ our comfort overflows. If we are distressed, it is for your comfort and salvation; if we are comforted, it is for your comfort, which produces in you patient endurance of the same sufferings we suffer. And our hope for you is firm, because we know that just as you share in our sufferings, so also you share in our comfort. (emphasis mine)

To summarize principle two then, God allows suffering in our lives to discipline, train, and grow us in the process of our sanctification. This process may consist of warning and disciplining us of our own sin and may also develop perseverance, character, humility, and sympathy so that we may endure suffering and experience the comfort of Christ in order to strengthen our faith and encourage others.

Now, notice that through the process of sanctification, we are increasingly conformed to the image of His Son (see Romans 8:29), and we are given opportunity and greater ability to share the comfort we have received through Christ to those who also suffer. This leads us right into the third principle: so that "[our] faith … may result in praise, glory, and honor when Jesus Christ is revealed" (1 Peter 1:7).

Principle #3

How does our faith through suffering bring praise, glory, and honor? How does this happen when Christ is revealed? And *when* will Christ be revealed? Ultimately, what I want to propose here is that God may allow us to suffer to provide an opportunity to live out our faith in a way that opens the door to share the truth of the Gospel. And the sharing of the Gospel tells people who Jesus is (i.e., "reveals" Him) and does result in praise, glory, and honor being given to God!

Now, I admit that God allowing hard things in our life for the purpose of sharing the Gospel is not an immediately apparent reason for suffering, is it? So let me draw this out a little through some rhetorical questions. What if through our endurance of suffering, we can display the example set by Christ? That's what we read later on in Peter's letter:

> But if you suffer for doing good and you endure it,
> this is commendable before God. To this you were
> called, because Christ suffered for you, leaving you

an example, that you should follow in His steps. (1 Peter 2:20–21)

What if by our patient and trusting countenance amidst suffering, people are prompted to ask us how we can have such an attitude—such hope? In that way, we can then be ready to point them to the reason for our hope. Like Peter says,

> But in your hearts set apart Christ as Lord. Always be prepared to give an answer to everyone who asks you to give the reason for the hope that you have. (1 Peter 3:15)

What if God asks us to endure suffering to give us an opportunity to tell someone about the suffering that Jesus endured such that we can have hope through Him? Could that be a way to reveal Jesus Christ to a neighbor, friend, colleague, or acquaintance?[161]

---

[161] The most common way this verse is interpreted is that the phrase in 1 Peter 1:7 "when Jesus Christ is revealed" is referring to the return of Christ and the "praise, glory, and honor" are viewed as commendations that will be received from the Lord on the last day. Now, I am not trying to refute this interpretation, as it is certainly true that faithfulness will be commended and rewarded (see Mathew 25:14-30 or 1 Corinthians 3:14, for example). And "praise, glory, and honor" will absolutely be the result when Jesus returns and all things are made right and new. I am simply offering another interpretation where our following Christ's example, as clearly exhorted by the apostle Peter (see 1 Peter 2:21), may be a way to "reveal Christ" through the sharing of the Gospel, which also results in "praise, glory, and honor." Further, I do believe this interpretation is possible within the grammar of the text as well as aspects of the broader context of the letter. I also think that this interpretation fits well with the denotation of purpose indicated by the Greek term *hina* earlier in the verse. All that being said, I have refrained from a more technically analysis in this section as my goal is not to pit these two interpretations against one another as if one is right and the other wrong. Hence, this section may seem short and lacking in depth. But I hope the use of rhetorical questions

Or let's look at this a little further. Part of our sanctification is to be "conformed to the image of [Christ]" (Romans 8:29) and to "become mature, attaining to the whole measure of the fullness of Christ" (Ephesians 4:13). This will require a transformation in us (see Romans 12:2) to make our "attitude the same as Jesus Christ's" (Philippians 2:5). Part of this will require suffering because Jesus Himself was "made perfect through suffering" (Hebrews 2:10, 18) and we come to a fuller knowledge of Christ when we share in the fellowship of His suffering (see Philippians 3:10). And if we are in fellowship with Him and His Spirit resides in us (see Ephesians 3:17), then when we follow His example of enduring suffering (see 1 Peter 2:21), our character reflects that of Christ's and thus could serve as a bridge to sharing the foundation of our hope and faith (see 1 Peter 3:15). In this way, we can be ready to point to the love He displayed through His work on the cross and His resurrection from the dead as the reason for our hope, our patience, our perseverance, our endurance, our love and Him as the example we follow.

What if we can "reveal Christ" in that way through our suffering? Could that be a possible reason that God asks us to endure suffering? So that through the power of His Spirit in us that we can minister to those around us. So that we share in the fellowship of His suffering such that we can sympathize with others (see Hebrews 4:15), walk alongside them, and demonstrate His love for them. Ponder those questions for now. We will explore this in more detail later in the next two chapters.

Let's tie this back to what we learned about the purpose of pain from the physiological problem. Remember that pain is experienced when there is a *threat* to us from either actual or potential injury and it prompts us to act. In general, it is a clear indicator that the world is fallen and the existence of evil, suffering, natural disasters, war,

---

will prompt readers to consider these ideas and each can then arrive at his or her own conclusion as to whether this is an accurate exegesis of 1 Peter 1:7.

famine, illness, disease, and pain are warnings of the threats posed to us in this world. But when suffering occurs to us individually, God can use that in specific ways for our good and the good of others (see Romans 8:28).

God can allow suffering to prompt us to evaluate our hearts and ask ourselves if our love for Him is genuine (see 1 John 3:24). It can lead us to "examine ourselves to see [test] if we are in the faith" (2 Corinthians 13:5). These are aspects of principle one: testing our faith.

Pain and suffering can also serve as a signal of threat warning us of actual or potential sin, as it brings us to repentance, and it can develop perseverance, character, humility, compassion, and sympathy as it aids in our sanctification. That is principle two.

But pain and suffering in our lives can also provide an opportunity to follow the example of Jesus Christ and allow us to demonstrate His patient endurance and provide a bridge to share the Gospel. Thereby, our suffering may provide an avenue to reveal Christ and to witness to others to bring praise, honor, and glory to God, which is principle three.

Can we see this? From this perspective, suffering can indicate either actual or potential threats to our soul, prompt us to action, increase our assurance in the authenticity of our faith, purify and refine us, and conform us more and more into the likeness of Christ! And through that conformity, perhaps we can reveal the truth of the Gospel of Jesus Christ to some.

I guess at this point, in my view, there is ample reason to believe what the apostle Paul says in Romans 8:28: "And we know that in all things God works for the good of those who love him."

In all things—even evil things, even hard things, even painful things—God can work for good. And He may just be doing it so that it trains us to yield a harvest of righteousness and peace (see Hebrews 12:10).

Now that we have laid out these three principles in succession, let's see how they have played out in practice by examining each of them in the life of a biblical character.

6

The Personal Problem in Practice

How long will you torment me and crush me with words?
Ten times now you have reproached me;
shamelessly you attack me.
If it is true that I have gone astray, my
error remains my concern alone.
If indeed you would exalt yourselves above me
and use my humiliation against me,
Then know that God has wronged me
and drawn his net around me.
Though I cry, "I've been wronged!" I get no response;
Though I call for help, there is no justice.
He has blocked my way so I cannot pass;
He has shrouded my paths in darkness.
He has stripped me of my honor and
removed the crown from my head.
He tears me down on every side till I am gone;
He uproots me like a tree.
His anger burns against me;
He counts me among his enemies.
His troops advance in force;

> They build a siege ramp against me and encamp around my tent.
> He has alienated my brothers from me;
> My acquaintances are completely estranged from me.
> My kinsmen have gone away; my friends have forgotten me.
> My guests and my maidservants count me a stranger;
> They look upon me as an alien.
> I summon my servant, but he does not answer,
> Though I beg him with my own mouth.
> My breath is offensive to my wife;
> I am loathsome to my own brothers.
> Even the little boys scorn me;
> When I appear, they ridicule me.
> All my intimate friends detest me;
> Those I love have turned against me.
> I am nothing but skin and bones;
> I have escaped with only the skin of my teeth.
> —Job 19:2–20[162]

Principle #1: The Prototypical Example—Job

Injustice. Depression. Despair. Anger. Hopelessness. Defeat. These are all words and emotions that we could use to describe the anguish being expressed by Job in this passage. Job is the prototypical example of unprecedented tragedy, pain, and suffering!

His story is arguably one of the oldest pieces of literature known to man. Although the precise date of writing is unknown, the story

---

[162] Forgive the lack of an introductory clinical story. Since this chapter consists entirely of examples from biblical stories, I felt that the use of another clinical story would be redundant. So we will focus on the case examples that God has given us in His Word to demonstrate each of the principles we discussed in the last chapter.

of Job may precede that of even Abraham.[163] The man has served as a paradox of suffering for millennia, has been a subject of study for ages, and is—just perhaps—such an old story because God wanted to provide us an example of pain and suffering to help us grapple with our own.

As we begin to look at the story of Job, a brief summary may be helpful. For those of you unfamiliar with the story or just needing a refresher, Job is a man who God allows Satan to bring all kinds of suffering to. In one day, Satan works through different means to have a neighboring tribe attack and steal his ox and donkeys, a fire destroyed his herd of sheep and the servants attending them, a band of robbers take all of his camels, and a windstorm levels the house where Job's sons and daughters were feasting and kills them (see Job 1:13–22). Despite this tremendous day of trial, Job still praises the Lord. Because of this, Satan ups the ante and strikes Job with sores all over his body (see Job 2:7–8). So, to add to the emotional suffering of losing his fortune and family, physical suffering through bodily ailment and pain has now been added to the mix! The rest of the story then moves into numerous dialogues as Job and some of his friends try to understand why Job may be experiencing such suffering.

As we dig into the book of Job, it is helpful to understand it from a ten-thousand-foot perspective first. The book opens and closes with a narrative of what is surrounding the story of Job on earth. We, as the readers, are provided a description of what is occurring in heaven in the presence of God in the first chapter (Job 1:6) and are provided a narrative summary of how Job's life ends in the last chapter (Job 42:16-17). But the thirty-nine and a half chapters that are written between these sections of the book capture the dialogue

---

[163] The proposed time period for which Job lived is thought to be sometime around the patriarchs, as noted in Concordia Self-Study Bible—New International Version (1984), edited by Robert G. Hoerber, Horace D. Hummel, Wlater R. Roehrs, Dean O. Wenthe. This is also noted in *The MacArthur Study Bible* (Nashville, TN: Thomas Nelson:, 1997).

between Job and his friends (chapters 3–37) and Job and God (chapters 38–41). These chapters are full of philosophical musings, theological assumptions, correct and incorrect statements, rhetorical questions, presuppositions, and accusations at each other and at God, some that are true and others that are false.

This makes reading through the book of Job and making sense of all that is being said really challenging. So if any of you out there are thinking, *I just don't get the book of Job. It doesn't make sense. What am I supposed to be learning from this?*, don't worry. You are not alone.

That being said, let's try to understand the main points of the middle section of the book where we understand the situation through the perspective of Job and his counselors and then look at it from the heavenly perspective as outlined for us in God's responses to Job and the opening and closing narratives.

OK, here we go!

So, chapters 3–37 consist of a long back-and-forth dialogue between Job in the midst of his suffering and his three—later four— friends who have come to comfort and counsel him. What these dialogues reveal is an underlying assumption that is thought to be the main question of the book: is God just?[164] And if God is just, then He must run the universe according to the principle of justice. The way they assumed this would be worked out is by God punishing evil and rewarding obedience to God—no exceptions.[165] Thus, Job must have done something to *justify* his suffering. He must be guilty before God. Why else would he be suffering so greatly? God punishes only evil, right?

What this reveals to us is that Job and his friends are operating under a *huge* assumption and a simplistic one at that. They assume that God runs the universe *strictly* according to justice. Thus, if one lives a wise and good life, success and reward will be the result. And

---

[164] "Job," The Bible Project, https://bibleproject.com/explore/video/job/

[165] See *Interpretive Challenges* in the introduction to the book of Job in *The MacArthur Study Bible*, 695–695.

if one lives an evil and foolish life, punishment, pain, and suffering will be reaped. We see this in the very first speech from Job's friend Eliphaz, which begins like this:

> Consider now: who, being innocent, has ever perished? Where were the upright ever destroyed? As I have observed, those who plow evil and those who sow trouble reap it. (Job 4:7–9)

What Eliphaz is essentially saying is that you reap what you sow. You are reaping suffering, so you must have sown some sort of evil. Now, this is not untrue, but it is also not universally true. But Job and his friends are working under the *assumption* that it is always—and universally—true and, therefore, applicable to everyone in every situation.

This assumption leads to a huge internal struggle for Job, because he maintains throughout the book a protest of his innocence (many of us, I'm sure, can relate!). In his last speech to his friends in chapter 31, Job lists off a series of questions asking where he might have gone wrong and then concludes in verses 35–37,

> Oh, that I had someone to hear me! I sign now my defense—let the Almighty answer me; let my accuser put his indictment in writing. Surely I would wear it on my shoulder; I would put it on like a crown. I would give him an account of my every step; like a prince I would approach him.

Job is crying out, "I have done all that I know how to do to maintain my righteousness. If I have gone wrong, show me! Yet I have received no answer. I would gladly give you an account of every step and action I have taken to understand where I have gone wrong or what I have done to deserve this, yet no accusation have I found."

Now, *we* know from the prologue that Job is right. He is, in fact, innocent. He is called righteous and blameless by God and lauded as living a life of honor (see Job 1:1). But Job is never informed of this. He is never given an explanation for his trials and suffering. Can you appreciate the struggle here?

Job is so confused and in not only physical but mental turmoil, because he can't understand what he has done that would lead God to treat him this way. This leads Job to question the underlying assumption of the book. Because Job is innocent, yet he is suffering greatly, either God is not just, or God does not run the universe *strictly* according to justice. There must be other reasons that God allows suffering.

However, every time Job pleads his case, one of his friends responds, "No, no. God is just, and He does operate according to justice, so you must have sinned. It's the only way that can explain the tremendous suffering that you are facing." And this argument goes back and forth for the entirety of these thirty-five chapters.

Now, even though that probably seems like a long portion of scripture devoted to describing an argument, the benefit of this is that we get to see the wide range of emotions that Job experiences through this—everything from confusion to anger, from despair to hope, sadness and bitterness, to joy and happiness. We even see Job accusing God of injustice and torment and ultimately demanding an answer from God! Whew! That's bold!

But if we remember the assumptions that Job and his friends are making about God—that because God is just, He *always* runs the universe according to *only* justice—we can understand Job's confusion, frustration, anger, and even his accusation of God. After all this, God provides His answer but probably not in the way Job, or any of us, would have expected.

So the next part of the book (chapters 38–41) provides us with God's *response* to Job, which actually never really *answers* Job's question. We do not see God giving Job a clear explanation for his suffering. What God does do is respond to Job through a series of questions—over sixty questions! Questions like: Where were you when I laid the foundations of the earth (38:4)? Have you ever given orders to the morning or shown the dawn its place (38:12)? Can you bring forth the constellations (38:32)? Who provides food for the raven (38:41)? Do you know when the animals give birth (39:1–4)? Essentially, God asks Job, "Who do you think you are? And who do you think I am? Look around at what I have created! You think you can do better?"

God thoroughly reminds Job of his place as a special creation of God, but one of limited understanding, power, and perspective. However, in all of this, He never tells Job why all this happened. God never explains to Job the reasons that He allowed it. Instead, He simply reminds Job of His power, glory, and wisdom, with the clear implication that Job is not in a position to challenge God but rather must *trust* Him.

So what was God's main message to Job? Remember *who* I am and *trust* Me even when, sometimes, it doesn't make sense to *you*.

Now, I know someone out there is thinking, *That's it! That's what you are going to conclude? Come on! What a cop-out answer! I want to know* why *God is putting me through this agony. Why He allows all the suffering in this world! I don't want some Sunday school answer, "Well, just trust God."*

Yeah, I'm right there with you. Sometimes the cliché answer, "Just trust God," doesn't seem very satisfying. But at the end of the day, it is true. And from Job's perspective, he had to fall back on that. But I think the book of Job has more to offer *us* than just that.

Let's zoom out again and consider Job's struggle in light of the extra detail *we*, as the readers of the book, are provided from the prologue and epilogue. Remember that in chapter 1 verse 6 the author of Job gives us a sneak peek into the heavenly realm. We read,

> One day the sons of God [also interpreted angels] came to present themselves before the LORD, and Satan also came with them. The LORD said to Satan, "Where have you come from?" Satan

answered the LORD, "From roaming through the earth and going back and forth in it."

Just a quick interjection to note a few things. First, this is a break in the text where the author is giving us, the readers of the book, additional detail and backdrop to the story. This is information that Job does not have as a person in the narrative, but we—as readers of the book—do have. And this is crucial information. What we see here is that there is a heavenly council that observes the earth and that there is a being—Satan—that roams back and forth in the earth. So let's keep this in mind—that there was and are heavenly beings that observe the earth and another being that roams throughout the earth—as we continue to read through the opening portion of the book.

All right, continuing in verse 8,

> Then the Lord said to Satan, "Have you considered my servant Job? There is no one on earth like him; he is blameless and upright, a man who fears God and shuns evil."

Pause! Right here, we have strong evidence that all of the dialogue we were just discussing in chapters 3–37 was based on a false assumption. All through that section of the book, Job's friends were accusing him of some sin—known or unknown—that Job must have committed to have resulted in him suffering so much. They are assuming that Job has done something that would deserve such suffering. But right here in this verse, we see *from the mouth of God* that this not the case! This is super important for us to remember as we interpret the book of Job. Job's suffering was not the result of divine *justice*.[166] Job was not being punished for some sin

---

[166] Although God is certainly just and does operate in accordance with justice, the case of Job is not a simple manner of "Job did x, y, or z; therefore, he is getting what he deserves." It is important to remember that God would

that he committed. He was not receiving retribution for his mistakes or failures. But it was the result of divine *purpose.*

So what was that purpose? Well, we are never told explicitly, but I think we can make a very reasonable inference from what follows next in the prologue to the book of Job. In verse 9, Satan says,

> "Does Job fear God for nothing? ... Have you not put a hedge around him and his household and everything he has? You have blessed the work of his hands, so that his flocks and herds are spread throughout the land. But stretch out your hand and strike everything he has, and he will surely curse you to your face."

Now, what is the basic accusation Satan is making here? He is saying, "Of course Job serves you! Look at how you shower him with gifts. Job isn't upright because he is devoted to you. He serves you because it benefits him. There is a lot in it for him to do what You say when the result is prosperity. His piety—his religiosity—it's a sham! It is just self-serving. He is just loving himself. Take all that away, though, and then we will see Job's true character."

This brings us right back to principle one in the personal problem of pain: God allows pain in our lives to prove our faith in, and love for, God as genuine, by causing us to ask the question, "Do we love *Him* or just the things He gives us?"

This is the heart of Satan's accusation against Job, isn't it? This is essentially what Satan is telling God about the "good deeds" and "uprightness" of Job. And what does God say in response to this claim?

In verse 12, we read,

---

still have been just to allow all this to happen to Job because of the simple fact that Job is sinful in his nature, but God viewed him as blameless and upright because he "fear[ed] God."

> The LORD said to Satan, "Very well, then, everything he has is in your hands, but on the man himself do not lay a finger."[167]

God essentially says, "OK. Let's see if you are right. Go ahead and test him, and we will find out if Job's service is *genuine*. We will see if his devotion is *authentic*. We will see if he has *faith* in *who* I am." Faith.

Remember what we read in 1 Peter to arrive at principle one?

> These [trials] have come so that your *faith* ... may be *proved genuine* (v. 7; emphasis mine).

This is exactly what is happening here with Job. He is being tested to prove that his *faith*, devotion, motivation, *trust*, reverence, and *love* for God are real. That they are authentic. That they are *genuine*. Thus, we see that pain and suffering can test us, like it did

---

[167] It is important to note here that the specific forms of suffering that Job experienced—the atrocities that happened to him—were the direct work of Satan. That the devil is at work to bring about suffering and temptation is a truth that we see affirmed later in the New Testament (see Ephesians 6:11 and 1 Peter 5:8). However, what this passage also indicates is that Satan needed to be permitted, by God, to do these things. So, is some suffering caused by Satan? It would appear so. Is Satan free to do whatever he wishes on earth? It would appear not. This raises all sorts of questions as to what the ultimate source of evil is, how this fits within God's sovereignty, and some may even see this as an affront to the character of God in wondering why He would allow Satan to do any of this. However, it is extremely important to remember that the character of God is clear in the Bible. He is loving and gracious, kind and merciful, righteous and good, while also just and holy and possesses wrath and indignation toward sin and evil. Yet the Bible is less clear on what the source of evil is and how the mechanics of God's sovereignty play out alongside people who have some capacity to make choices. This is a topic closely related to pain and suffering but one that deserves special attention. Thus, I only mention it here to acknowledge its role, but I will not try to address it within this book.

Job, and can serve as a warning of the subtlest forms of a wayward and idolatrous heart.

Does that make sense? Can we see that? When we find ourselves challenging God because He has allowed something to be taken from us, we may need to evaluate our faith. Look at how Job responded right away to his trials:

> Shall we indeed accept good from God and not accept adversity? (Job 2:10 NASB)

Job's faith and devotion to God remained intact, and he acknowledged that this did not depend on what he "accepted" or received from God, thus implying that his faith was grounded in who God was, and ultimately, this experience only increased Job's knowledge of God's character—as we shall see in a little bit. So I hope that we can understand the danger of loving God for the good things He can give us and the pleasures He can bestow upon us and how that can be confused with love for *Him*. And I hope we can see the value in having that tested.

But having said that, I imagine someone is thinking, *OK, OK. I get how that could be true for Job. But he was a special case. This sort of thing doesn't happen anymore. We aren't tested before the council of God.*

Actually, the Bible does allow us to make a case for this. Take a look at Ephesians 3, verse 10:

> His intent was that now, through the church, the manifold wisdom of God should be made known to the rulers and authorities in the heavenly realms.

Did you catch it? Let's read it again.

> His [God's] purpose was that *now* [that is this present age—the times in which we live], through *the church*

123

> [the church as in the assembly of believers—that's you and me], the manifold wisdom of God should be *made known to the rulers and authorities* [this phrase is often interpreted as angelic beings] in the heavenly realms [where? To rulers on earth? No. In the heavenly realms]. (emphasis mine)

Well, that kind of sounds like what was described in Job chapter 1 and verse 6 where an assembly of angels presented themselves before God. And then God used a person who believed in Him (like a person in His church) to demonstrate an aspect of His wisdom. Hm, yes, very similar.

And if we read further in Ephesians, chapter 6, verse 12 says,

> For our struggle is not against flesh and blood, but against the rulers, against the authorities, against the powers of this dark world and against the spiritual forces of evil in the heavenly realms.

"Not against" what? Not against flesh and blood. But against what? Spiritual forces. Forces where? In the heavenly realms.

So, yes, the type of testing and trials that Job suffered, endured, and experienced can and does happen to believers today. And it can happen to me and to you. But remember its *purpose* can be to prove your faith—my faith—our faith as *genuine*. And that faith is of greater worth than gold and therefore worth suffering for.

So, again, let's repeat principle one in the personal problem of pain: God allows pain in our lives to prove our faith in, and love for, God as genuine by causing us to ask the question, "Do we love Him or the things He gives us?"

Now, the next question, then, is how do we know that this is the principle that is applying to our particular situation?

Oof, that is the tricky part. We can't just assume that we are being tested in this way because there are at least two other principle purposes that may be at work here! So how do we know if this is what is going on in our case?

Well, at the risk of letting you all down, I don't believe we will ever know—for sure. Why do I say that?

Because that is what seems to happen in the story we are considering.[168]

Let's return to the book of Job and look at God's response to Job. In all of chapters 38, 39, 40, and 41, which give us God's response, Job is never given an explanation. God never tells Job why. He doesn't even inform Job of the heavenly council, of Satan's accusation of him, or of this being a test. Nor does God encourage Job by telling him that this story will serve as a source of encouragement, an example of endurance, a *prototype* of righteous suffering for thousands of years to come! No. All God asks Job is, "Who am I?" Followed by, "Who are you?"

God asks Job,

> Would you discredit my justice? Would you condemn me to justify yourself? Do you have an arm like God's, and can your voice thunder like his? (40:8–9)

Now, that is not to say that God won't illuminate our spirits and our minds with an answer, but it is to say that we cannot demand a full or complete explanation. Nonetheless, we can *trust* Him that there is one. Right? That's one of the points of the whole book of Job. There was a very important reason that Job was suffering. But to prove Satan wrong, to prove that Job's service and devotion and love for God was genuine, Job had to arrive at the point of simply trusting *who* God was. And that includes *trusting* Him even when

---

[168] Certainly, from the implications of this story and 1 Peter 1:6–7, we can be reasonably confident that this principle is at work to some degree in all instances of suffering, but we can't necessarily assume that this, and only this, is why God is allowing suffering in our particular case.

he didn't have all of the answers—even when he didn't completely understand.

So God does give a response that I think is both instructive to Job and for us. Look what God says to Job's friends. Starting in verse 7 of chapter 42, we read,

> He [God] said to Eliphaz, "I am angry with you and your two friends, because you have not spoken of me what is right, as my servant Job has …"

Wait! Job spoke rightly of God? But he was all over the place! He was up, down, inside out, and twisted in his emotional turmoil over his pain and suffering. He accused God of injustice. He rebuked the counsel of his friends. He spoke harshly. He dipped into despair, depression, and hopelessness. And you say Job was right?

That appears to be what *God says,* right? And God not only says it, but he repeats it. In verse 7, God tells Eliphaz that Job has spoken rightly, and then He says it again in verse 8:

> "You [Eliphaz] have not spoken of me what is right, as my servant Job has."

Well, that is very interesting, isn't it?

What should we take from this? We will get into this in more detail in chapter 7 when we discuss the pastoral problem of pain, but the short answer is that those emotions that Job expressed—anger, sorrow, confusion, despair—are real. They are valid. They can, and arguably should, be felt. There is nothing wrong with those emotions in and of themselves. We need not feel guilty for having them. We are not less spiritual if we have to wrestle with them for a while. We are not unsaved if they are quite prominent when walking through a difficult time.

Yet even though there is nothing wrong or sinful in having them, what we *do* with them is very important. So here is the instructive part for us. When we look at all the outbursts, confessions, discourses, and dialogues put forth in the book of Job, there is a very important distinction that should be made. Job repeatedly directed his emotions, thoughts, outbursts, and complaints *to* God. He didn't distance himself. He didn't walk away. He didn't "curse God and die" like his wife suggested. No. He turned *to* God—over and over again. Even when God didn't seem to be answering, he kept going back.

In his first speech, Job says, "Remember, *O God*, that my life is but a breath" (7:7; emphasis mine).

He addresses God. His second speech opens with him framing all of his questions in the context of comparing himself to God! He says, "But how can a mortal be righteous *before God*?" (9:2; emphasis mine).

In his third speech, he keeps his thoughts directed toward God as he announces, "*To God* belong wisdom and power; counsel and understanding are his" (12:13; emphasis mine).

And then later, he requests *of God*, "Withdraw your hand … to let me speak, and you reply (13:21–22).

In chapter 19, he clings to hope and cries out,

> And after my skin has been destroyed, yet in my flesh I will *see God*; I myself will see him with my own eyes—I, and not another. How my heart yearns within me!" (v. 26,27; emphasis mine)

Again and again, he pours out his soul *to* God. He beseeches and searches *for* God in the midst of his suffering.

So what do we learn from this? Well, God said that Job was right in doing this! And if we continue to turn to God—to lean into Him and lay our thoughts and emotions before Him, to *pray* through our suffering—I believe that we will get a response. That response may not be a complete explanation or the exact answer that you were looking for, but I do think it will be a response full of hope. Look at the result for Job. In Job's final reply to the Lord, he says, "My ears had heard of you, but now my eyes have seen you" (42:5).

Now my eyes have *seen* you ...

By the end of the book, Job didn't get an explanation. He got something better. He received a revelation—a revelation of the *person* of God. He received what He cried out for in chapter 19. He was granted the experience of knowing and loving God for who God is and received a greater knowledge and experience of Him! And he was essentially given another life after the trial—just like we are promised a new life after our trials here on earth.

And with that, perhaps the words of the apostle Paul in 2 Corinthians 4 may make more sense:

> Because we know that the one who raised the Lord Jesus from the dead will also raise us with Jesus and present us with you in his presence. All this is for your benefit, so that the grace that is reaching more and more people may cause thanksgiving to overflow to the glory of God. Therefore we do not lose heart. Though outwardly we are wasting away; yet inwardly we are being renewed day by day. For our light and momentary troubles are achieving for us an eternal glory that far outweighs them all. So we fix our eyes not on what is seen, but on what is unseen. For what is seen is temporary, but what is unseen is eternal. (v. 14–18)

We do not lose heart. We trust that our afflictions—our momentary troubles—are working toward purifying our heart, such that we know God, such that we trust God, and such that we *see* God (see Matthew 5:8).

So it is that one of the principles of our personal pain is that God allows pain in our lives to prove our faith in and love for Him as genuine by causing us to ask the question, "Do we love Him or the things He gives us?"

Next, we will look at principle two: God allows pain in our lives to discipline, correct, train, teach, and sanctify us. To help understand this, we will be studying the character of David—the punitive example.

Principle #2: The Punitive Example—David

Have mercy on me, O God, according to your unfailing love;
According to your great compassion blot out my transgressions.
Wash away all my iniquity and cleanse me from my sin.

For I know my transgressions, and my sin is always before me.
Against you, you only, have I sinned and
done what is evil in your sight,
So that you are proved right when you speak and
justified when you judge. (Psalm 51:1–5)

Hear the cry of lament from a man broken by his sin and suffering because of it. A man who realized that many of the trials he faced were a consequence of his own doing. Psalm 51 is the cry for mercy and forgiveness after the unfolding of a story of betrayal, adultery, conspiracy, murder, and tragedy comparable only with modern-day Hollywood. This is the cry of David—an anointed king over Israel, the conqueror of a giant, the hero of a nation, the defeater of tens of thousands, and a man of grave sin. Yet the only man in the entire Bible described as one "after God's own heart" (Acts 13:22).

The story of Job demonstrated—in great detail—how God can use our suffering to *test* us (principle one). The life of David is an example of how God can use our suffering to *teach* us (principle two). Our suffering can be used in the process of sanctification in telling us of our sin, cleansing us from that sin, and directing us toward righteousness. In a sense, our suffering can be punitive. Not punitive strictly in the sense of punishment as a retribution but punitive in the sense of a consequence imposed for the purpose of punishment,[169] discipline, correction, and/or instruction.

Let's review the story of David to see how this principle plays out. So David was the youngest of eight brothers, the sons of Jesse. He tended his father's sheep in the hills of Bethlehem. After King Saul had disobeyed God, Samuel was instructed to go to the house of Jesse to offer a sacrifice and anoint the future king who would take Saul's place (see 1 Samuel 16:1). It was David who God saw had a heart He desired for the king of his people (see 1 Samuel 16:7).

Samuel anointed David, and the Spirit of God came upon David. David was then appointed to serve as a minstrel in Saul's court to ease the king when "tormented by an evil spirit." David served in this way by going back and forth between his father's fields and the king's court until a challenge was put forth by the champion of the Philistines, Goliath of Gath. David was completing his rounds between his father's house and King Saul when his father instructed him to check on his brothers at the battle field. Here is where the famous David and Goliath story takes place.

David accepts the challenge of the Philistine and defeats him with only a stone and sling. He receives wide acclaim and is appointed to remain in the king's court from then on (see 1 Samuel 18:2). David becomes a loyal and successful servant of

---

[169] I use the word *punishment* here with some reservation. I mean this only in the sense of a negative consequence imposed as a result of a wrongful action, with the goal of deterring that action from happening again. This is consistent with psychological use of the word *punishment*. The judicial use of the word *punishment* is the infliction of a consequence to serve as a retribution. Now the retribution for sin is death (see Romans 6:23), so I do not have that sort of punishment in mind here. So, to be absolutely clear, when I refer to *punishment*, I am only using this in the sense of a negative consequence meant to deter sinful behavior consistent with a form of discipline.

the king and is lauded by the people—"David has slain tens of thousands!" (see 1 Samuel 18:7). This sparked an intense jealousy and suspicion of David that would remain for the rest of King Saul's life.

David is then given command of a thousand men, has many successful campaigns against the enemies of Israel, and is offered the hand of marriage to two of Saul's daughters (he eventually accepts the second offer in response to a proposed price for the hand of Michal). David's continued success only incites further jealousy and rage from the king, which ultimately results in him ordering his commanders to kill David. This is followed by a long period where David flees Saul as his rage against David grows. Eventually, David is positioned on two occasions where he could have killed Saul but did not, reasoning to himself, "I will not lift my hand against my master, because he is the LORD's anointed" (1 Samuel 24:10).

After Saul's death, David becomes king of the house of Judah, and more fighting breaks out between those loyal to David and those loyal to Saul. Eventually, David is anointed king over all Israel (2 Samuel 5:3). David then leads Israel on several successful conquests against the neighboring nations and recaptures Jerusalem. God even blesses David, promising him a great name, that his house and kingdom will be established, that he will have children to succeed him, and that he will build a house for the Lord (see 2 Samuel 7:3–16).

Note here that David's life has been blessed. He is clearly in the favor of God and men (minus Saul of course). He has lived with integrity and honor. He has remained faithful to God and to King Saul despite very challenging times. And his military conquests have been amazingly successful and blessed by God (see 2 Samuel 8:14). He has quite the spiritual acumen! But he is not above failure. He is not above discipline and chastisement, even though chosen and blessed by God (see 1 Samuel 16:7 and 2 Samuel 7:5–16).

After years of success and an illustrious life as king, David perhaps gets a little too confident—a little too comfortable in his status of blessing. In 2 Samuel 11, the Bible outlines a descending spiral of events that ends with tremendous suffering for David, his family, and the nation.

In verse 1 of chapter 11, we are told that David stayed in Jerusalem when he customarily would have gone off to battle. Now, we are not given the specifics as to why David stayed behind, but it wasn't due to the absence of war, because we are told that David sent Joab and the whole army in his stead. But, for whatever reason, David broke with custom as king and remained at his palace—one small step off the straight and narrow. As he was strolling about the roof of his palace, his gaze caught the sight of a beautiful woman— Bathsheba, the wife of Uriah (who was a loyal friend of David's). David sees her bathing and—boom! Before we know it (within three verses), David sends for her, sleeps with her, and impregnates her!

David then proceeds to try to cover up the affair by sending for Uriah (bringing him home from battle) and entices him to sleep with his wife (two times unsuccessfully!). As he is unable to make it look like Uriah is the father of the child, he then conspires with Joab (commander of the armies) to place Uriah in an area of fighting to ensure he is killed, thus playing party to murder. This is quite the series of events for a man described as "being after God's own heart" to be engaged in!

Now, let's just recap here. At this point, David has had a successful campaign of military conquests, kingly rule, and moral integrity of approximately forty-five years,[170] and in a matter of months, he commits adultery, betrays a trusted friend, conspires with military leaders, and murders a faithful servant. Although this was done in secret, these sins did not go unnoticed by God (see 2 Samuel 11:27).

---

[170] William H. Gross, "Chronology of David's Life," 2005. Retrieved from https://hpbcwiw.files.wordpress.com/2019/02/190129-chronology-of-davids-life.pdf. Accessed November 3, 2022.

So God sends the prophet Nathan to confront David. Let's pay careful attention to what the Lord says through Nathan:

> Why did you despise the word of the LORD by doing what is evil in his eyes? You struck down Uriah the Hittite with the sword and took his wife to be your own. You killed him with the sword of the Ammonites. Now, *therefore*, the sword will never depart from your house, *because* you despised me [God] and took the wife of Uriah the Hittite to be your own ... Out of your own household I am going to bring calamity upon you. Before your very eyes I will take your wives and give them to one who is close to you, and he will lie with your wives in broad daylight. You did it in secret, but I will do this thing in broad daylight before all Israel. (2 Samuel 12:9–12; emphasis mine)

Note the use of *therefore* and *because*. These indicate that God's judgment was a *consequence* of David's actions (principle two).

David then acknowledges his sin (2 Samuel 12:13) and repents (see Psalm 51), but look at how Nathan replies to this:

> The LORD has taken away your sin. You are not going to die. But because by doing this you have made the enemies of the LORD show utter contempt, the son born to you will die. (2 Samuel 12:13–14)

God took away David's sin, but He did not remove all of the consequences of that behavior. The child dies, David has marital conflict and domestic challenges for the remainder of his life, his own sons fight among each other, and one of them even tries to usurp David's thrown and causes the kingdom to divide! But it is extremely important for us to remember that even though the consequence remained, the sin did not; God took the sin away (2 Samuel 12:13). So, in light of our second principle in personal suffering, yes, we are forgiven. Yes, we live in an age of grace. Yes, we can and must repent of sins. Yes, we will never achieve sinless perfection in this life. But God is also holy and just, and the sin of confessing Christians profanes God's character and must be cleansed. We are disciplined for sinful behavior, for the protection of God's character and for our good.

I think at this point it is good for us to read Hebrews 12:5–11 in light of what we are currently discussing.

> And you have forgotten that word of encouragement that addresses you as sons: "My son, do not make light of the Lord's discipline, and do not lose heart when he rebukes you, because the Lord disciplines those he loves, and he punishes[171] everyone he accepts as a son."

> Endure hardship as discipline; God is treating you as sons. For what son is not disciplined by his father? If you are not disciplined (and everyone undergoes discipline), then you are illegitimate children and not true sons. Moreover, we have all had human fathers who disciplined us and we respected them for it. How much more should we submit to the Father of our spirits and live! Our fathers disciplined us for a little while as they thought best; but God disciplines us for our good, that we may share in his

---

[171] Note the word *punishment* here is in line with the sense used throughout this section: a negative consequence for the purpose of deterring the repeating of a negative behavior. Not punishment in the sense of a consequence to serve as final retribution.

holiness. No discipline seems pleasant at the time, but painful. Later on, however, it produces a harvest of righteousness and peace for those who have been trained by it.

God disciplines and punishes (v. 6) us not because we have fallen from grace but because He is showing us grace. He is treating us as His children! Because He loves us. Because He desires good for us. Because He is training us to share in His holiness. And this process is painful at times. So this can happen in a positive sense, building us up (as we will be discussing in principle three). And it can happen in a negative sense, breaking us down and revealing to us our sin (as we see in the life of David). But there is an important distinction we must take note of when considering God's discipline as *punishment* or chastisement for sin, and the story of David illustrates this well.

David's sin did not condemn him (cf. Romans 8:1), but his sin did lead to chastisement and suffering. Not only did this protect God's reputation, but it corrected David and redirected his life and behavior. David was clearly a man blessed of God and one in a position of prominence and great influence over God's literal earthly kingdom. Because of that, God could not allow David's behavior to provide opportunity for anyone to show contempt to His character (see 2 Samuel 12:14), and God did not allow David to continue down the path of dishonesty and treachery he began to follow (for David's sake and for Israel's sake).

And the Lord's correction did its work. Look at what David writes later in his life regarding the Lord's discipline:

> Cleanse me with hyssop, and I will be clean; wash me, and I will be whiter than snow. (Psalm 51:7)

> Restore to me the joy of your salvation and grant me a willing spirit, to sustain me. Then I will teach

transgressors your ways, and sinners will turn back to you. (Psalm 51:12–13)

Though you have made me see troubles, many and bitter, you will restore my life again; from the depths of the earth you will again bring me up. You will increase my honor and comfort me once again. (Psalm 71:20–21)

Before I was afflicted I went astray, but now I obey your word. (Psalm 119:67)

It was good for me to be afflicted so that I might learn your decrees. (Psalm 119:71)

As we learn God's decrees and obey His Word, we increasingly reflect His character and share in His holiness. We are sanctified! And God's discipline of our sinful behavior is one means of that being accomplished. It "cleanses" and "washes" us (Psalm 51:7) and "produces a harvest of righteousness and peace for those who have been trained by it" (Hebrews 12:11).

So, yes, suffering can be a result of our sins. The immediate question on our minds right now is "How do we determine if this is the case? How do I know if my suffering is because of my own sin?"

This is both a really hard question and really important question to ask, but I won't be able to answer this question for you on the pages of this book. I would say that this is something you are going to have to figure out individually. This is a question that I can only answer by asking God for myself, and you can only answer by asking God for yourself. I can't tell you the inner workings of your heart—like we read in 1 Corinthians:

Who among men knows the thoughts of a man
except the spirit of the man which is in him? (2:11
NASB)

But God does give us some direction and instruction in how we can do this. In 2 Corinthians, we are told, "Examine yourselves to see whether you are in the faith; test yourselves" (13:5).

This examination is to test whether we are—what? In the faith. Sometimes our trials are present to do—what? Prove our faith (remember principle one) and to see if we are living according to that faith (principle two).

Well, what does this examination look like? Prayerful, careful, and honest. This must be done with God and balanced with an understanding of the deceptiveness of our own hearts. Because we will likely be tempted to try to jump to the conclusion that we are "upright and blameless"—like Job—without taking a close and clear look at our own heart.

So an important step is to pray as the psalmist:

Examine me, O LORD, and prove me; test my
mind and my heart. (Psalm 26:2 NASB)

Or like we read in the concluding remarks of Psalm 139,

Search me, O God, and know my heart; test me
and know my anxious thoughts. See if there is
any offensive way in me, and lead me in the way
everlasting. (139:23–24)

This examination must include an invitation to the Lord to help us, as it is the Lord who will reveal this to us—even if that is through the confrontation of a brother or sister in Christ. Remember David understood the gravity of his sin only after God sent a prophet to rebuke him!

Then, once we turn to God, we must remember that we really need Him to reveal our hearts to us. Remember that "the heart is deceitful above all things" (Jeremiah 17:9) and that "all the ways of a man are clean in his own sight, but the LORD weighs the motives" (Proverbs 16:2 NASB).

Therefore, we will need God to examine us (see Psalm 26) and search us (see Psalm 139), and He has provided us His Word to guide us in this. Consider Hebrews 4:12:

> For the word of God is living and active. Sharper than any double-edged sword, it penetrates even to dividing soul and spirit, joints and marrow; *it judges the thoughts and attitudes of the heart.* (emphasis mine)

So I believe that when we turn to God and we search His Word, we can have confidence that "if we ask anything according to His will, He hears us" (1 John 5:14 NASB).

We know that it is His will to save sinners (see Luke 19:10; 1 Timothy 1:15). Thus, when we come to Him asking to be saved from sin (even unknown sin), we can be confident that He hears us. Because of this, I believe that when we approach God in this way and kneel in His presence through prayer, He will move in our hearts to either convict us of that sin and reveal it to us (because it is His will to save sinners from their sin) or clear our conscience and make us confident that this is not due to sin and assure us. Verse 15 of chapter 5 in 1 John goes on to say,

> And if we know that he hears us—whatever we ask— we know that we have what we have asked of him.

Since being saved from sin is God's known will, when we pray to be saved from our own (even in the sense of becoming aware of it to repent of it), I think we can be confident that this is a prayer that is according to His will. He therefore hears it and thus will grant the request to us. Because of that, I believe God will show us any sin for which He is disciplining us for, so that we may confess it and repent of it. That does not necessarily mean that the pain or suffering will be immediately removed (remember David still suffered the consequences of his sin), but we would at least then know part of its purpose—warning us of the threat of unknown sin to lead us to repentance. It may very well also be serving to grow us in other ways, however.

To recap, principle two shows us that God can use pain and suffering as a consequence for a particular sin or to cleanse us in the way of bringing us to repentance and making us more holy. But we must remember that God disciplines us as His children for our good and so that we can become more like His Son, Jesus. It is part of the work of *sanctification*. This sanctification process has a negative component where we are confronted and brought to grips with our own sin, yes. But there is another aspect of this as well. The other side of the sanctification process is to train us in righteousness to reflect God's character. This part of the sanctification process is where we see an overlap between this principle and the next—that we may "reveal Jesus Christ" to others (principle three). So the positive aspect of sanctification—training in righteousness, growing in humility, teaching us sympathy, and so on—will be discussed under the next section.

Principle #3: The Preeminent Example—The Apostle Paul

> Therefore I urge you to imitate me. (1 Corinthians 4:16)

The apostle Paul stands out in several ways. He did not walk with Jesus during His life. He is the only apostle who had prominence in the Jewish Sanhedrin. He is the apostle with the most impressive academic pedigree. He is the apostle who wrote the majority of the

New Testament, penning more books than any other. Thus, he is preeminent or distinguished in many ways. Yet even he understood that he was not "preeminent" in the sense of "surpassing all others," "of paramount rank" or of "chief importance." No, he clarifies elsewhere that the true preeminent example is that of Christ. He writes in 1 Corinthians 11:1, "Follow my example, as I follow the example of Christ."[172]

So in its truest sense, the preeminent example of suffering is Jesus Christ. But Paul lived a life as a disciple of Christ, showing us how we are to follow Christ's example and thereby be conformed to His image (see Romans 8:29). Thus, it is through the life of Paul that we see one of the best (the preeminent) examples of how we (as disciples) are shaped and molded and formed into an increasing Christlike character through suffering that may allow us to reveal the character and message of Christ to others (principle three).

We are first introduced to the man we now know as the apostle Paul in Acts 7, where we are told the witnesses of the first Christian martyring laid their clothes at the feet of a man by the name of Saul (v. 58). This man was there "approving" the stoning of Stephen (Acts 8:1). As we continue to read the book of Acts, we gather bits and pieces of who this Saul character was. We learn that he was determined to "destroy the church" (v. 8:3). He even went directly to the high priest to attain the authority to imprison anyone professing to follow Christ (Acts 9:2). And his zealous rage against the disciples of Jesus is described as "murderous" in Acts 9:1.

Then when he is on his way to Damascus to search out and "destroy" the Christians there, he has a miraculous encounter with Christ Himself (Acts 9:4). From this point on, we see a dramatic change in this man's character. So much so that at some point in his ministry, he changes his name and is later referred to as Paul (see Acts 13:9), perhaps to illustrate his change in heart.

As Paul becomes increasingly prominent and instrumental in

---

[172] This is also affirmed by the apostle Peter in 1 Peter 1:21.

the spread of the Gospel, we gather more and more information about who he was and who he became. We understand that he was from Tarsus (Acts 9:11; 21:39) but was raised in Jerusalem (Acts 22:3). While there, he studied under and was trained in the Jewish law by the most prominent rabbi of the time (arguably of all time)— Gamiliel (Acts 22:3). He eventually became a Pharisee (Acts 23:6) and potentially a member of the Sanhedrin (see Acts 26:10–11).[173] His frequent citations of Greek poetry and philosophy also suggest that he was extremely well educated academically and potentially skilled in politics.

Yet after his encounter with the risen Christ on the Damascus road, a complete change occurs in him. We see him going from a raging persecutor of the church to one of its most zealous evangelists and defenders within a span of a few years (see Galatians 1:17–18). He goes from sentencing Christians to prison to being imprisoned on their behalf! He goes from deriding the person of Christ to aspiring to be more and more like Him. What a change!

Although the transformation that we see in Saul of Tarsus becoming the apostle Paul was instigated by the call of Jesus Christ, it was perfected through suffering. Paul being "conformed to the image of [Jesus]" was completed through hardships, challenges, hurts, betrayals, and pain. He writes to the Philippians that part of the knowledge of Christ that he was acquiring was "the fellowship of sharing in his [Jesus's] suffering" (Philippians 3:10).

And Paul was no stranger to suffering! In defending his authenticity as an apostle, we see a rare instance of Paul listing his own experiences and circumstances in 2 Corinthians 11:23–33. Here he lists having been imprisoned on more than one occasion, having been flogged, on the verge of death, received "the forty lashes minus one" five times, beaten with rods three times, stoned once,

---

[173] See John MacArthur, *The Gospel According to Paul* (Nashville, TN: Nelson Books, 2017, p. xiv) for a defense of this passage as support of Paul's membership in the Sanhedrin.

shipwrecked three times, floated in the open sea for over a day, and been in danger of multiple threats! Paul knew what it meant to hurt, to suffer, and to anguish. Yet he did not bemoan these experiences. He actually praised God for them, as they showed him his weakness (v. 30).

But this did not occur without a struggle. Later on in that same letter to the Corinthians, Paul gives us a personal insight into his own struggle with some of his suffering when he describes his "thorn in the flesh" (12:7–10). We are never told specifically what this thorn was, but we are told that it "tormented" Paul (v. 7). He also writes that he pleaded with the Lord that it would be removed, but it was not. The Lord allowed it and left it for a purpose—to "keep [him] from becoming conceited" (v. 7), to teach him to rely on God's grace (v. 9), and *so that*[174] Christ's power would rest on him (v. 10).

From this, we can see that Paul is not being punished for a specific sin (the thorn was not placed punitively); rather it was to "keep him" from entering into sin and help him remain humble—like Jesus (see Philippians 2:3–5), to rely on God's grace—like Jesus (see Matthew 4:4), and that Christ's power would be evident in him (v. 9–10). It was through his suffering that Paul learned more and more about the suffering of Jesus and was transformed and conformed to be more and more like Him, which is what he writes earlier in that same letter to the Corinthians:

> We … *are being transformed into his [Jesus's] likeness* with ever-increasing glory, which comes from the Lord, who is the Spirit. (3:18; emphasis mine)

It was because Paul knew this that he was able to face his sufferings with peace and joy. Remember in Romans 5, he writes:

---

[174] The Greek in verses 7 and 9 is *hina*. See discussion in the previous chapter and the etymology of this word and its denotation of purpose.

> But we also rejoice in our sufferings, because we know that suffering produces perseverance; perseverance, character; and character, hope. And, hope does not disappoint us, because God has poured out his love into our hearts by the Holy Spirit, whom he has given us. (v. 3–5)

It is suffering that builds our character and leads to a greater knowledge of God's character. And God's character is exemplified in Christ (see Hebrews 1:3), and that love is demonstrated through Christ (see 1 John 3:16). And our suffering helps in the process of transforming us into the likeness of Christ (see 2 Corinthians 3:18).

Paul recognizes this idea in writing to the Philippians when he says that through sharing in suffering, he may "become like him [Jesus] in his death" (Philippians 3:10). So understanding and sharing in suffering conforms us to—makes us like—Jesus, even unto His death. It grows us in our character and our humility. It allows us to sympathize with those who are also suffering (see Hebrews 4:15) and to be a source of comfort to them (see 2 Corinthians 1:3–7). Then, when others see us suffering with joy, with grace, with peace, and with hope, they may be prompted to ask us how we do it. And then we can be "ready" with an answer (see 1 Peter 3:15).

That answer is of course that we live in hope and peace, even in the midst of suffering, because we have an example of one who went before us. We have a hope of everlasting life. We know that there is a life beyond this world and that heaven awaits us because of the example of selfless, loving, enduring suffering that went before us— our Lord and Savior Jesus Christ. Through that kind of "answer," I propose that it is through the suffering in our own lives that we may be able to 'reveal Jesus Christ' (1 Peter 1:7) to others (principle three).

Paul puts the principle this way:

> We always carry around in our body the death of Jesus, so that the life of Jesus may also be revealed

> in our body. For we who are alive are always being given over to death for Jesus' sake, so that his life may be revealed in our mortal body. (2 Corinthians 4:10–11)

Paul was acutely aware that God worked through trials and challenges—pain and suffering—to reveal the character of Christ and to show His grace and power. It was for this reason that he could say, "Therefore I will boast all the more gladly about my weaknesses, so that Christ's power may rest on me" (2 Corinthians 12:9). So, just like the Apostle Paul, we have a very real opportunity to demonstrate to people the character of Christ—to reveal Jesus Christ in our body—in the way that we endure suffering. This is yet another reason that God may allow trials of all kinds in our lives. Our suffering and the way we compose ourselves in that suffering may demonstrate the character of Christ to those around us and lead to an opportunity for us to share our faith and the message of the Gospel to others. Is this not a tremendous reason to allow suffering? Is this not something we can be joyful for, to have the opportunity to serve the Lord and work for His purposes?

Perhaps this is a perspective on suffering that many have not considered before. And I hope and trust that considering this as a reason God may allow suffering in your life may prompt you to look for opportunities to share His truth and grace with others.

But let's recap. Through Job, we see how God can allow pain and suffering as a *test* of faith—to prove it genuine. Through David, we see that pain and suffering can come as a result of our own sin and to *teach* us, to discipline us, to bring us to repentance, and to aid in our sanctification. And through Paul, we can see that God can allow suffering to *transform* us and make us more like His Son so that "Jesus may be revealed in our body" and we can share the hope we have in Christ with whoever may ask us the reason we have for hope—even in and amidst great pain and suffering.

Now that we have a greater understanding of why pain and suffering may occur, the next question is, what do we do with it? When we, or those around us, are experiencing it, how can we help them? That's what we will address in the next two chapters as we look at the pastoral problem of pain.

7

The Pastoral Problem—Helping in Pain

I was working on some documentation in the office one day when one of our newly hired therapists came to consult on a patient with me.

"I am working with a young man who is recovering from a shoulder dislocation that happened almost three months ago," she said, "and I am having a really hard time getting his range of motion back."

"How have you treated it so far?" I asked.

"Early on, just gentle range of motion, but over the last several weeks, a lot of manual therapy and stretching. But what's weird is that I can get his arm into end-range positions, but he gets this consistent shaking in his arm when I pass a certain point in his range of motion," she responded.

"What kind of resistance do you encounter? Is it a tissue barrier, or does it feel like guarding—like he is just resisting you from moving his arm farther?" I asked, trying to understand the clinical situation more clearly.

"It just feels like his arm is … is shaking. He says he can't control it, and it hurts into the back of his arm down past his elbow and sometimes into his thumb."

"Not in his shoulder?" I asked, just to make sure.

"No. He doesn't have much pain in his shoulder at all anymore. His pain is almost always in the back of his arm."

"How does he describe the pain?" I asked with increasing suspicion that we were dealing with something more than just a shoulder dislocation.

"He says it shoots from the back of the shoulder to his elbow, and then it kind of burns," the therapist responded with a look of a little confusion, as she was probably reacting to the increasingly noticeable furrowing of my eyebrows.

"Does he have any neurological symptoms? Numbness, tingling, weakness?" I asked.

"Well, I guess I'm not sure about those symptoms now, but now that you mention it, he did say that he had a lot of tingling the first few weeks after the injury."

"Aaaahhhh," I said, putting another piece into the puzzle of this patient problem. "I don't think we're dealing with a shoulder joint issue."

"What do you mean?" the young therapist asked a little incredulously. "He had a clear dislocation! It took over four hours for him to be able to get the help he needed to have it reduced!"

"Yet another piece of information that only supports my hypothesis," I calmly replied as I was relishing this opportunity for a teaching moment. "How much background did you get (before coming here) on pain mechanisms?"[175]

"Not much," she admitted.

"OK. I think this will be important to understand in directing us where to go with your patient, so let's take a crash course in pain

---

[175] *Pain mechanism* is a concept that is becoming accepted more and more among health care providers and researchers. The basic idea is that not all pains are created equal. Different kinds of pain can arise through different processes, or mechanisms, in our body. And understanding which process is driving a person's pain will lead to different treatment and management of that pain. So identifying the underlying mechanism of pain is an important step in selecting the appropriate response and treatment.

science and discuss the different mechanisms that are currently agreed upon. The International Association for the Study of Pain endorses three broad categories of pain: nociceptive, neuropathic, and nociplastic.[176] Nociceptive pain is pain that arises from a normally functioning sensory nervous system. For example, there is an injury—or tissue damage—that activates sensory nerves that relay a signal to the brain that activates an internal alarm system to alert the person of threat or injury. Neuropathic pain is pain that arises from a specific form of damage occurring in nerves. This can happen in the periphery or in the central nervous system. Neuropathic pain has a distinct presentation from nociceptive pain in that it is usually accompanied with neurologic symptoms and has quality and description often accompanied with pins, needles, burning, numbness, or shooting, electric-like sensations. Further, this will usually have a distribution that matches a peripheral nerve or dermatome.[177] And nociplastic pain is the pain that arises when something within the nervous system is leading to altered processing of sensory signals. This is pain that arises when there is no clear evidence of damage or threat to the body or nervous system.[178]

"Returning to your patient, is there evidence of damage to his body?"

"Yes," came the immediate reply from my new colleague.

---

[176] "Terminology," Resources, International Association for the Study of Pain, accessed July 10, 2020, https://www.iasp-pain.org/terminology?navItemNumber=576#Nociplasticpain.

[177] A dermatome is an area that is supplied by different nerves that all converge to the same place in the spinal cord. That is, the nerves are supplied by the same root from the spinal cord.

[178] Ruth L. Chimenti, et al., "A mechanism-based approach to physical therapist management of pain," *Physical Therapy* 98, no. 5 (May 2018), 302–314, https://doi.org/10.1093/ptj/pzy030. Keith M. Smart, et al., "The discriminative validity of "nociceptive," "peripheral neuropathic," and "central sensitization" as mechanisms-based classifications of musculoskeletal pain," *Clinical Journal of Pain* 27, no. 8 (October 2011), 655–663, https://doi.org/10.1097/AJP.0b013e318215f16a.

"Right. So it is very unlikely that we are dealing with a nociplastic pain. But does he have neurological symptoms?" I asked, hoping to lead her down a path of reasoning through these symptoms she hadn't considered yet.

"Well, not anymore, but he did at first," she replied, but still without the confidence I was hoping for.

"Right, so he had clear neurological symptoms at first. But what about the distribution of his pain that you described to me earlier? He gets symptoms down the back of his arm, into his lateral forearm and thumb and lateral hand, right?"

"Yeah! Which is so weird. I would expect his pain to be located around his shoulder because of the injury sustained there!" she responded with some enthusiasm, being affirmed that her thoughts of an atypical presentation were accurate.

"Yes, that is an unusual pattern of symptoms to come from the shoulder joint. But does that distribution make sense for a different structure?" I asked. Not waiting for her to reply, I prompted her further. "Does that match a muscular referral pattern, joint referral pattern, dermatome, or peripheral nerve distribution?"

"Peripheral nerve?" the therapist answered, still without the confidence and conviction I was hoping for.

"Right. That pattern matches almost perfectly the areas supplied by the radial nerve, right? So is it possible that when his shoulder was dislocated for four hours, while the bone was out of joint, it either put direct pressure on or tensioned the radial nerve to the point that it could have been injured?"

"Oh yeah! I didn't even think about that." Her face lit up in such a way that indicated she was catching my drift and following the line of reasoning I was directing her in.

"So if he has a possible nerve injury, what kind of pain are we probably dealing with? Nociceptive or neuropathic?" I asked, returning to our discussion of pain mechanisms.

"Neuropathic."

"Exactly. And if this is a neuropathic pain arising from an

injured nerve (or nerves!), will we want to stretch and mobilize the joint in positions that may place stress on those injured nerves?" I asked, trying to connect the dots between accurate diagnosis and appropriate treatment selection.

"No!" she answered with an air of understanding and relief of having a clearer direction to go to help this patient. "We will want to gently work into that and not cause much provocation of symptoms and inform him that this will be a much slower process to heal from than just a joint dislocation because nerves take much longer to heal."

"Absolutely!" I replied. "We need to adjust our strategy based on the *mechanism* that is driving his pain."

Just like in the clinic where treatment should hinge on accurate diagnosis of disease, injury, and pain, the way that we help people in the midst of pain and suffering should reflect our understanding of that person's specific circumstances. We should handle the question "Why is there pain and suffering in the world?" differently when a college student is asking us this question over a cup of coffee than we would if a friend or relative is asking us this after losing a child. This is hopefully intuitive and without need for a thorough defense, but I am repeatedly surprised at how often I hear academic answers being given to people who are in the midst of deep suffering. Don't get me wrong; there are times and places that an academic answer that delves into all the different philosophical approaches to reconciling the existence of pain and suffering with God's good purposes is appropriate, but we need to do our best to discern when that is the case.

So here is what I think is important for us to understand. When we are answering the question "Why do we hurt?" it is imperative to determine what perspective the question is coming from. Is the question being asked simply to understand the apparent conflict in Christian doctrines and just come to an intellectual treatise between the idea of a loving God who allows tremendous suffering? Or is the question coming from someone who is trying to understand personal pain, grief, or loss?

If the question is coming from intellectual and philosophical motives, then we answer the question philosophically and have a discussion to clarify aspects of the person's worldview and beliefs about the nature of the world, God, man, sovereignty, morality, destiny, and so on. Providing a guide into these discussions is a book in and of itself and outside the scope of what I aim to write here, but there are excellent resources that exist for guidance in this area, and readers can refer to chapters 2 and 3 of this book for some understanding of the more academic side of this question.

However, if the person is in the midst of personal suffering, our approach to this should be different. The approach to helping people in the midst of suffering may not even utilize academic or intellectual answers at all! It may just consist of a sympathetic presence and compassion for the person in their suffering.

Now, as we continue in this chapter, at the risk of disappointing many of you, I am not going to present a step-by-step process that we can follow in order to help people in pain. The reason for that is I don't know that one exists. Rather, I am going to return to the idea we have been discussing in the last two chapters—that different principles may be at work in a person to explain their suffering—to build the case that helping people to try to understand how God can be using their experience of pain for His purposes can be very helpful. Because of that, I am going to present, as best I can, how the Bible instructs us to help in each of those different circumstances.

The last thing I want to mention before jumping into the content of this chapter is that if you—or a friend or family member—are suffering from physical pain, please consider seeing a health care provider.[179] We went to a lot of school and spend a lot of time

---

[179] I will also clarify that my personal opinion is that you should have a firm trust in that health care provider. If you walk away from your initial

studying physiology and the effectiveness of different interventions in order to help people who are suffering. And many of us will encourage you to pray and seek the Lord through this. Many of us will also pray that the Lord would heal you physically, emotionally, and spiritually. Many of us try to practice our profession within a biblical framework of ultimately trusting God yet using the minds He has blessed us with to understand how natural and man-made things may facilitate the physiological processes of healing that God has created to help things along. So seeking the counsel of a trained professional is not an act demonstrating a lack of trust in God—as some people may believe. Rather, it can be an act of trusting God when He says, "In an abundance of counselors there is victory" (Proverbs 11:14 NASB).

With that as an introduction, how do we help people who are in pain or going through a period of suffering? How do we care for them through this? This is the challenge we face when seeking to guide—or shepherd, as the Bible refers to it—people. The term *pastor* is the Latin term for "shepherd." It comes from the idea of leading to pasture—to lead to nourishment, refreshment, and

---

consultation with him or her feeling wary of their advice, either go back and clarify or get another opinion. You are under no obligation to stay with any provider just because you saw that person first. I don't think anyone would disagree that having confidence and trust in your provider is a very helpful thing in seeing a positive outcome. This is known as *therapeutic alliance* within health care and has been recognized in numerous fields from physical therapy and physical pain (Folarin Babatunde, et al., "Characteristics of therapeutic alliance in musculoskeletal physiotherapy and occupational therapy practice: a scoping review of the literature," *BMC Health Services Research* 17, no. 1 (May 2017), 375, https://doi.org/10.1186/s12913-017-2311-3.) to psychotherapy and emotional pain (Daniel J. Martin, et al., "Relation of the therapeutic alliance with outcome and other variables: A meta-analytic review," *Journal of Consulting and Clinical Psychology* 68, no. 3 (June 2000), 438–450.

safety.[180] The difficulty in discerning how we do that is the pastoral problem of pain.

In trying to provide some general principles that we can follow to help people (others or ourselves) through a time of suffering, I want to emphasize clearly at the outset that how these are applied will depend heavily on the circumstances at hand. I would encourage all of us to seek the Lord and pray for wisdom on how to navigate any of the situations that we individually encounter. My hope is that what follows is a helpful resource for thinking through how that may look.

To start, I would encourage all of us to recognize the value of just being there with someone. When we see someone suffering, offering our presence is an important first step. Look at the story of Job.

> When Job's three friends, Eliphaz the Temanite, Bildad the Shuhite, and Zophar the Naamathite, heard about all the troubles that had come upon him, they set out from their homes and met together by agreement to go and sympathize with him and comfort him. When they saw him from a distance, they could hardly recognize him; they began to weep aloud, and they tore their robes and sprinkled dust on their heads. Then they sat on the ground with him for seven days and seven nights. No one said a word to him, because they saw how great his suffering was. (Job 2:11–17)

There are several things we can note from this passage.[181] First of all, Job's friends were moved to compassion. They "heard about

---

[180] See entries under "pastoral" and "pastor" in the Online Etymology Dictionary, accessed March 24, 2021, www.etymonline.com/word/pastoral and www.etymonline.com/word/pastor.

[181] I fully recognize and acknowledge that this is a narrative passage and is therefore not instructive in the sense that it is imperative that we follow this example. But I think it is a vivid illustration of a repeated theme that we see

all the troubles that had come upon him," so they literally moved—"they set out from their homes"—in order to "sympathize with him." So there was an acknowledgment of the reality of the situation, which prompted compassion and sympathy. Then their goal was to ease Job's suffering; they set out to "comfort him." And to do that, "they sat on the ground with him for seven days and seven nights." They were literally and physically present *with him*.

So when we see someone in pain and suffering, let's acknowledge the reality of that pain and suffering. Admitting to ourselves and to the person who is hurting that the situation is, indeed, difficult can communicate and initiate the process of our desire to understand the situation and help. And part of doing this may be to allow ourselves to feel the hurt with that person. We see that Job's friends "began to weep aloud." This is consistent with what we read in Romans 12:15: "Mourn with those who mourn."

Yes, that may be uncomfortable, but it can be a profound source of help. And it can communicate to the person that we actually want to be there *with* them. It helps us to offer our presence, our support, and our prayers.

Next, we should notice that Job's friends "sat on the ground with him for seven days and seven nights. No one said a word to him." Job's friends were just with him. They didn't offer counsel. They didn't offer condolences. They didn't offer explanations. They just sat there "because they saw how great his suffering was."

What this shows us is that when we see someone in the midst of tremendous suffering and we are feeling and thinking, *I have no idea what to say*, it is perhaps quite appropriate to say nothing. In fact, it was only after Job's friends each opened their mouths and offered their thoughts and explanations for his situation that Job calls them "worthless physicians" (Job 13:4) and "miserable comforters" (Job 16:2).

---

throughout the Bible that is consistent with God's repeated reminder that He Himself is with us in trials and suffering (see Isaiah 43:2–5).

That is not to say that we should never say anything but only to validate that our presence is indeed sometimes a help in and of itself. And this has actually been shown to some degree within medical and psychological studies. Having a diverse social network that offers support and companionship has been linked with a variety of different health outcomes.[182] In understanding how our relationships affect health, I want to point out just a few things that studies have suggested may implicate why having companionship through interpersonal relationships may be so helpful.

First, feelings of loneliness have been linked to poorer immune function[183] along with anxiety and depression.[184] Further, the sense of loneliness is not necessarily linked with actually being isolated.[185] What I mean by that is a person may actually have people in his or her life who are available. In other words, the person is not physically isolated from people, but he or she may still feel lonely. People may perceive themselves as being alone in the difficult situation they are facing even when they have a social network available to them. So it's not just important to have people around to offer support but actually having someone available to talk to about the pain, the suffering, the challenges that the person is facing.[186]

This leads us to another thing that appears important regarding

---

[182] Sheldon Cohen, "Pyschosocial stress, social networks, and susceptibility to infection," in *The Link between Religion and Health: Pyschoneuroimmunology and the Faith Factor*, ed. Harold G. Koenig & Harvey J. Cohen (New York: Oxford University Press, 2002).

[183] Ibid.

[184] Nancy J. Donovan, et al., "Loneliness, depression and cognitive function in older U.S. adults," *International Journal of Geriatric Psychiatry* 32, no. 5 (May 2017), 564–573, https://doi.org/10.1002/gps.4495.

[185] Timothy Matthews, et al., "Social isolation, loneliness and depression in young adulthood: a behavioural genetic analysis," *Social Psychiatry and Psychiatric Epidemiology* 51, no. 3 (March 2016), 339–348, https://doi.org/10.1007/s00127-016-1178-7.

[186] James W. Pennebaker, et al., "Disclosures of traumas and immune function: Health implications for psychotherapy," *Journal of Consulting*

companionship and how it can be helpful. Actually listening to a person and allowing them to express their grief openly is an important part of offering support and help to a person.

What these studies show is that having people around to help truly has an influence on how the situation is perceived, how the situation is handled, and the behaviors that are adopted to manage, process, and (hopefully) persevere through the challenge. So making an attempt to simply offer your presence and support—even if you can't provide answers—is in and of itself a very real means of help in the midst of pain and suffering.

To summarize, the principles we see from Job's friends is that being moved to offer our presence, our compassion, and sympathy are very helpful things. We also see that being quick to speak and offering presumptuous explanations are often not helpful and can actually be hurtful.

Now if we do feel compelled to offer counsel or explanation in some way, it is very important that we first listen very carefully in order to ascertain what principle of pain is potentially at work in the person's life. This is what Job's friends did not do. Job expresses his turmoil in chapter 3, and Eliphaz responds immediately with a presumption that Job is "reaping" what he has sown (Job 4:8). To remain consistent with the illustration outlined at the beginning of this chapter—pain mechanisms—Eliphaz did not do his due diligence in reasoning through multiple potential reasons that God could allow suffering. Rather, he assumed the suffering was punitive. This is a mistake that may lead to hurting those we are trying to comfort—like Job's friends did to him.

To avoid this, we must listen carefully and understand the situation as best we can. Or as James puts it in his epistle, "Everyone should be quick to *listen*, slow to speak" (James 1:19).

We must remember that the person who knows the most about

and Clinical Psychology 56, no. 2 (April 1988), 239–245, https://doi.org/10.1037//0022-006x.56.2.239.

the situation is the person going through it. The person who knows the depths of the sorrow and grief and all the raging emotions and thoughts is that person (cf. 1 Corinthians 2:11). So we do well when, in wisdom, we try to draw the matter out of the person as one would draw water from a deep well (Proverbs 20:5). The best source of information regarding the situation is the person themselves, so it is reasonable, at the right time, to ask questions. These questions can serve as the bucket that retrieves the water from the well of the heart.

And one important question that may often be overlooked is, does the person even want help? Are they looking for counsel or assistance? Or do they simply need to express their sorrow and grief to someone? Do they need someone to help process their emotions to determine if they are valid and justified? Or do they need someone to help encourage them to move forward?

This is rarely apparent on the surface. So in discerning what a person is looking for, we can follow what we have covered so far: acknowledge the reality of the suffering, offer your presence, feel the weight and pain of the situation with the person (which may be the first step in validating their emotions[187]), and then after all of that, begin to ask questions with the intention of listening.

Perhaps an open-ended question like "What can I do to help?" or "What is it that you need right now?" is the simplest way to start. Who knows. They may just say that they need someone to get them a coffee. Then you just find the closest coffee shop and get them their favorite frilly coffee drink, and your job is done! Nonetheless, starting with questions will begin to clarify what the person needs and how you can help and if you can help.

Then let them fully disclose the situation to you—as much of it as they are comfortable sharing anyway. Don't jump in with quick answers or jump all over them with correction if they express

---

[187] Not all of a person's emotions will necessarily be valid, however. So there may be times when we need to confront a friend or person. We will touch on those types of situations later.

something that makes you feel uncomfortable. Let the person express the situation and the feelings associated with it so that you understand as fully as possible. Then you may offer correction if that is needed, express sympathy if that is indicated, or offer encouragement if that seems to be the most appropriate thing.

As you are listening carefully and compassionately, the details of the situation may help to clarify a few things—both for you and the person. This is where I want to draw our attention back to pain mechanisms. During this process, I am going to suggest that another layer of discerning how to help is to consider what type of suffering the person is going through and what principle of pain may be working in the person's life in discerning how we can best shepherd this person. Or how we can lead or assist this person to a refreshing pasture, if you will.

This would mean that as we are understanding the situation, it is reasonable to ask, "Is this person's suffering a test proving their faith, is it a result of their own actions or sin, or is this something that is pruning their character?" We then respond accordingly.

When Trials Are a Test

To some degree, any type of pain and suffering is serving as a kind of a test, so in one sense, pain is always acting in this way. Remember, the genuineness of a person's faith will be clarified in the presence of pain and suffering (see 1 Peter 1:7). In these situations, our main role is to listen, understand, sympathize, observe, remind, and encourage. As just mentioned previously, we will not know how to respond unless we have thoroughly listened to the person in order to understand the situation. And if, from that, our best discernment leads us to a conclusion that this person is not reaping what they have sown in a negative sense, then I think it is reasonable to conclude that this is serving as some kind of a test of faith or training their character. For our current consideration is when this is a test of faith.

After we have listened and understood such that we feel confident that this is a test of faith, we can sympathize and then observe. Let's not try to point out the silver lining with statements like "Well, at least this or that didn't happen" or "It could have been worse" or just with a glib "God works all things for good."[188] Rather, we are called to feel the situation with them—"mourn with those who mourn." Be there for them and let them know that you care.

Then when we are present with them, we can observe. And what I would suggest that we observe is how they are responding. If we see that they are questioning things about God, such as His goodness or His sovereignty, that would be a time to remind them of the many truths about God and the many promises He gives to those in this world—especially to those who are going through trials. On the other hand, if the person is already turning to God and expressing faith in Him through their suffering, I think we only need to offer a hearty amen and continue to encourage them and seek ways to offer support to any physical or practical needs that arise.

Now, I imagine that someone reading this is asking, "What truths and promises are we to remind people of when they begin to question God?" Let me start to answer this question by reminding us that when we are facing trials as a test, it is a test of our faith. Remember in 1 Peter we read that it is our *faith* that is being proved genuine. Ultimately, when a person's suffering causes them to begin to wonder something like "Is God really good?" or "Is God really in control of this situation?" it is their faith that is being tested because they are being placed in a position where they are unsure of the truth of something that God has said about Himself. So the antidote here is to believe what is true.

---

[188] Although this is certainly true, my point here is that when we just throw that verse out there without consideration, recognition, and sympathy, this can feel more hurtful than helpful to the person, as it can communicate a lack of willingness to engage in the situation with the person because it can give the impression of a sort of indifference toward the real difficulties and struggles the person may be facing.

Jesus, when comforting His disciples during the Last Supper, says, "Let not your hearts be troubled. Trust in God; trust also in me" (John 14:1). Why were the disciples not to be troubled? Because they could trust—have faith and believe in—God. And this trust, this faith, is all encompassing. It is a faith that understands who God is and trusts what God has said about how He works in this world.

Then it is also important to remember that later in this very same discussion with His disciples, Jesus also tells them that "in this world you will have trouble" (John 16:33). So Jesus has explicitly told us to expect troubles, difficulties, challenges, disappointments, trials, pain, and suffering. But He reassures us that we can "take heart" because He has "overcome the world" (v. 33). Thus, despite experiencing troubles, we are not to let our hearts *be* troubled, because we can trust that God—through Christ—is sovereign and has overcome the troubles of this world. Here is the ultimate source of peace. A sort of peace that surpasses understanding (Philippians 4:7).

So we understand and believe that Jesus, as the Son of God, is our sovereign Lord (Jude 4), that He is the Almighty who declares the "beginning from the end" (Isaiah 46:10). That He knows all that happens in His creation—the thoughts we have (Psalm 139:2) and even the number of hairs on our head (Matthew 10:30). That nothing happens outside of His will even the death of a sparrow (Matthew 10:29). That even the hard things that happen to us God means for good (Genesis 50:20; Romans 8:28). That He will accomplish His purposes (Isaiah 46:11), which includes bringing His children into His presence as He goes to prepare a place for them (John 14:2–3). And that He demonstrated His power to do all of this by conquering death through His resurrection from the dead (Romans 1:4; Ephesians 1:20). When we believe all this, truly there is nothing that can separate us from the love of Christ (Romans 8:38–39), and we need not *be* troubled even in the face *of* troubles, because we can trust God's working in this world because He has shown us that He can use hard and terrible things to accomplish His purposes through Jesus's death on the cross (Acts 2:23)! And by looking at the cross, we can be assured of God's love for us because He gave His own life to save us (1 John 3:16).

This leads us right back to Jesus's words in John 14:1, "Let not your hearts be troubled. Trust in God; *trust also in me.*" When we understand all those things about God—His sovereignty, goodness, and love and His working of all things for our good—and then we also trust in His Son, who has demonstrated God's love for us—who has demonstrated that God has power over the grave, and who has promised to send us His Spirit—we can be confident that when we go to Him when we are weak and weary, He will comfort us and give us rest (see Matthew 11:28–30). We can have this rest because we know that, no matter what, He is with us (see Psalm 23), and He promises to never leave us or forsake us—especially in the midst of our troubles (see Hebrews 13:5).

That's why we can have a peace "that surpasses understanding." We don't need to understand all of the details of exactly *how* God is working out His purposes through what we are experiencing, because we *can* trust—and *must* trust—that God *is* working through whatever it is that we are facing for His purposes. In that way, we have an opportunity to remind ourselves and others of how the Gospel is the power of God to save those who *believe* (Romans 1:16)!

Now, considering all of that, what's the best way to find out if we really believe all of these things about God and His Son, Jesus? Well, for many of us, it will take the refining fires of trials (see 1 Peter 1:6–7). Difficult times, pain, and suffering will force us to really wrestle with these truths about God and will either drive us toward Him or will reveal our unbelief. Knowing that, when it comes to helping others, after we have listened, understood, sympathized, and observed, if we see someone struggling with these truths, we remind them of these truths. If we see someone struggling with the emotions of their situation but turning to these truths for comfort, we encourage them (which we will come back to). If we see someone beginning to deny these truths, we correct them, which is what we will discuss next.

When Pain Is Punitive

At the outset, I want to say that this is a very challenging truth that has some nuance to it. There seems to be this notion out there that nothing uncomfortable could ever be from God[189] or that God no longer brings upon us consequences for our sin. We live under grace, right? Although it is certainly true that we do live under grace, it is also true that we are in the process of being transformed, and we are still in the midst of a struggle with our sin (see Romans 7:14-25) and the powers and principalities of the air (Ephesians 6:12). And because of that, there is still refining going on. There is still an inward struggle with our sin. And it is still true that God will not be mocked, and we are being transformed into His likeness. Because of that, God's grace does not simply wink at our sin, just like a father does not just hug his son when he steals a piece of candy from the convenience store. A good and loving father implements a punishment, chastisement, discipline, and correction to return the erring child to the path of righteousness and to teach his son of the dangers and repercussions of theft. So we do need to recognize that there are times that the pain we suffer can be brought about directly or indirectly by God, because of our own foolish, careless, or sinful actions.[190]

---

[189] This is actually quite contrary to what we read in scripture. Isaiah 45:7 quotes God as saying, "I make peace and create calamity." Also, in Isaiah, God is described as one who "will bring disaster" (Isaiah 31:2). Then in Amos, we read, "If there is calamity in a city, will not the LORD have done it?" So the Bible affirms that hard things do come from God at times to bring about His purposes. That does not make these things morally evil when God is exercising judgment because "all have sinned" (Romans 3:23) and "there is none righteous, no, not one" (Romans 3:10), and thus justice sentences us all to death (see Romans 6:23).

[190] It is not my prerogative to make this determination as a health care professional in a clinical setting. Further, I almost never have enough information about a patient's life outside of the clinic to be able to evaluate this with any degree of accuracy. So I am in no way implying that clinicians

Tim Keller explains this idea as follows: "One kind of suffering is directly caused by our own failures."[191] Keller goes on to give an example of a career-driven woman who is ruthless and cruel in order to gain career advantage and suffers the loss of friendships. Another example would be the grief and relational turmoil brought on by marital infidelity. This idea is another way of expressing the punitive nature of pain and suffering we discussed through the story of David. There appears to be a type of suffering that God allows that is a result of our behavior, meant to serve the purpose of directing our attention to an area of our life that needs to be addressed. It is punitive in the sense that it is a form of punishment that is meant to bring repentance and change (see 2 Corinthians 7:10). Tim Keller puts it like this:

> Imagine that a man becomes engaged five times in a row, and each time he breaks up with his fiancée. Because each fiancée exhibits some personal flaw, he assigns the blame in every case to her faults. But actually, his own perfectionism and attitude of moral superiority are the main causes of the relationship failures. It is a huge blind spot for him. It may be, then, that one particularly brutal break-up might shake him to the core, and finally show him what he has been contributing to all this misery. His suffering and distress is a wake-up call to change something very particular in his life.[192]

should attempt to determine if a patient's pain is possibly due to sin in his or her life. I am only stating that when we are discussing this theologically, this seems to be a possible reason that God could use pain and suffering in the lives of people who may need to be corrected by the Christian brothers and sisters who are in close fellowship.

[191] Keller, "The varieties of suffering," *Walking with God through Pain and Suffering*, 207

[192] Ibid, 208–209.

As another example in the realm of physical pain (as opposed to emotional) is a father trying to complete an ultra-endurance event even though he has small children at home and his training is consistently taking him away from the family for multiple hours every weekend. This may be an abdication of his responsibility toward his family. If that is the case, I would suggest that it is sinful for that father to devote so much time and energy to his own recreational pursuits at the cost of investing in, caring for, and nurturing his family. This would also be known as selfishness. Thus, if he were to experience a nagging tendinopathy during the course of his training, I think it is reasonable to consider if that injury was ordained by the Lord to reorient that man's priorities—to serve as a wake-up call to change.

What we want to do here is acknowledge the possibility of pain and suffering being a result of people's own behavior. I don't want to imply that this is always the case. In fact, we want to be very careful in considering these as possibilities. But if we are drawing out the situation and listening carefully, I believe this will become increasingly clear if we are dealing with something like this. And if we are confident that sin is playing a role, this would be the time to implement correction and/or rebuke.

The words of Galatians 6:1 are both instructive and helpful here:

> Brothers, if someone is caught in a sin, you who are spiritual should restore him gently. But watch yourself, or you also may be tempted.

This verse points out a few things we want to ponder and check within our own spirit prior to offering any form of correction. And at the outset, I want to acknowledge that confronting people is challenging and can be hurtful, so we should do this with caution and care. We should observe that the first phrase of this verse is framing us into what kind of situations correction and confrontation are necessary for. And those situations are when "someone is *caught* in a *sin.*"

There are two things that we want to understand from this before going any further. One, we want to do our best to be sure that the person is *caught*. And second, we want to make sure that the thing the person is *caught in* is a sin. With respect to the first, we will want to consider if this is the first time something like this has happened—or has this become a habit? Is the person characterized by this, or does it only happen on rare occasions? For example, if your roommate in college just got pressured into his first drinking escapade and is feeling the effects this morning, you may just want to see if he learns his lesson from his hangover before jumping into a righteous rebuke. But if this becomes a Saturday-morning series, then he is demonstrating that he is getting *caught* in this reckless and sinful[193] behavior. This would then be the time for confrontation with the aim of restoration.

Really, this second point is happening along with the first, but we also want to be sure that our concern is truly over something sinful. Confronting someone over habitual drunkenness is an easier example because this behavior is explicitly stated to be sinful within the pages of scripture. But many behaviors are not so clear. Let's return to our example just a few paragraphs ago about the father training for an ultra-endurance event. Is it sinful to participate in endurance events? No, not inherently. Can it be sinful to participate in these events? Yes, I believe so. When does this cross the line into sin? When the motives are wrong or priorities have been misplaced.

Let's flesh this out a little further for the sake of clarity. If a person is simply participating in a race or competition (of any sort) to demonstrate their athletic prowess, to be frank, this is simply a combination of pride and selfish ambition. That is sinful. If a person is participating in an event because a coworker or neighbor or family

---

[193] Note here that the sinfulness of this behavior is the drunkenness (see Galatians 5:21), not the drinking.

member recently did a similar event and they don't want that person to be seen as doing something that they cannot do, that is envy. This is also sinful. If a person is competing in an event because they derive so much of their identity and self-worth out of their training regimen and ability to complete such events, so much so that they are willing to forgo other responsibilities (such as tending to the needs of the family on the weekend), that is idolatry. This person has just made it a priority to serve his self-interests over serving and obeying God. That is functionally placing one's self in the position of God and effectively breaking the first commandment. This is idolatry[194]—which is sinful.

Now, that I have successfully scared everyone reading this into never wanting to participate in any competition ever again, I want to clarify and reiterate that competition and participation in athletic events is not *inherently* sinful. There are many good and pure reasons that people may do this. They may simply enjoy the activity. They may enjoy the social aspect of it and meeting people. They may see it as an opportunity for evangelism. They may use it as a way to motivate themselves and others to exercise for health. Or they may participate because it is a charity event. So there are many good and right reasons to do these things. My intention is simply to point out that there are also sinful reasons that can worm their way into our hearts in these things. And we should be mindful of that, "examine our own hearts," and ask the Lord to "search our hearts" and "test our thoughts" to "see if there is any evil way in us" when it comes to these things.[195]

However, there may be a time when you become concerned that someone you know is getting caught in one of those sinful motivations. This would then be the time that, as a brother or sister

---

[194] Please see Colossians 3:5 for the scriptural basis for equating the pursuit of sinful desires to idolatry.

[195] This would be a good time to read 2 Corinthian 13:5 and Psalm 139:23–24 to let the Word of God do its work to judge our hearts (Hebrews 4:12) and show us our sin by looking into the mirror of the perfect law (James 1:25).

in Christ, you may need to speak into this matter. And if you believe this is necessary, this verse gives helpful guidance in how to do that.

Jumping ahead to the second sentence of verse 1, we read, "but watch yourself." In other words, check your own heart. Make sure that your desire is to *restore* this person, not simply to rebuke them to demonstrate your own moral superiority. Our desire should be from a heartfelt concern over the person's spiritual, physical, and emotional well-being. This is not always as easy as we probably think it should be.

It is both interesting and unfortunate that this verse warns us that we may be tempted during this process. This should be very sobering to us, as it seems to indicate that our sin can interfere with and tempt us even during acts of obedience, such as attempting to correct and confront someone who is in sin. Because of that, we want to heed the Word here and watch ourselves, or as verse 4 further clarifies, "each one should test his own actions."

So, putting this into practice, we should discern our motives and ensure that our aim is to restore. We should then look at our own lives and see if we are sinning in a way that may be seen by others. Remember the words of Jesus when He says to remove the plank from our own eyes before attempting to help dislodge a speck from someone else's (see Matthew 7:3–4). This doesn't mean that we have to be sinless in order to offer correction or rebuke, but it does mean that we should be very aware of our own struggles with sin, so that when we confront others, we can do this with a spirit of gentleness, just like Galatians 6:1 says—"restore him *gently*."

And that gentleness will be apparent when we approach a time of correction seeking first to understand the situation, being careful to draw conclusions, being prayerful as to whether what we are seeing in another person is habitual sin, watching and examining our own hearts, and then setting out to confront the person from a sincere desire to help and restore them. If we can honestly say that we are doing all of that, I believe that we will be "keeping in step with the Spirit" (Galatians 5:25) and He will give us the fruit of gentleness needed (Galatians 5:23).[196] Then we can help this person carry their burden of sin to the foot of the cross for forgiveness and through that act of love fulfill the law of Christ (Galatians 6:2).

When Suffering Is Sanctifying

At this point, if we are walking with someone through a painful time and they are repeatedly demonstrating their faith and trust in God and there is no obvious sin that seems connected to the issue that has not been repented of, it is reasonable to conclude that the primary function of the person's suffering is to grow their character (i.e., to sanctify them).[197] And in these situations, I believe our main role is to encourage.

We see multiple passages in the New Testament admonishing us to encourage one another and build each other up.[198] So when we see someone persevering through adversity, this is certainly an appropriate time to do so! Affirming their faith, complimenting the character qualities you see exemplified through their walk, and

---

[196] It is noteworthy that leading up to Galatians 6:1 is an entire passage of scripture instructing and admonishing us to live according to the Spirit, which is the context of the verse instructing us to confront someone in sin. I take this as a strong indication that our ability to do this well—gently—and actually lead someone to repentance and restoration will be largely contingent on us leaning on the guidance of the Holy Spirit during this process. We will need God's help to show us our own sin, discern our motives, see into the issue clearly, and remain humble and gentle throughout the process. So in the actual process of living this out, I would expect we would spend far more time in prayer and preparation for confronting someone than we spend in the actual act of talking with them.

[197] Obviously, the testing of faith and the bringing about of repentance are elements of sanctification as well. What I mean to do here is to highlight the element of sanctification that is dealing with the growth of other aspects of one's character.

[198] Just a short list of such verses includes Romans 14:19, 15:2; 2 Corinthians 12:19; Ephesians 4:29; Colossians 4:6; 1 Thessalonians 5:11; and Jude 20.

expressing the appreciation you may have for the example they are being to you and others are all simple ways to help that person see God working through their trial.

In addition to all of that, I think another way we can strengthen people is to encourage them to try to recognize opportunities to reach others through their trial. And here I would like to turn our attention to 1 Peter 3:15. We read,

> But in your hearts set apart Christ as Lord. Always
> be prepared to give an answer to everyone who asks
> you to give the reason for the hope that you have.

This verse is often quoted in the context of apologetics and used to support efforts to find and provide rational and intellectual defenses for the Christian faith. Now, I do think this verse supports those efforts, but I think if we understand this verse in only that way, we are missing something very important that the apostle Peter is communicating to us.

We have to remember that the entire epistle that Peter is writing is to Christians who are suffering persecution from the Romans. It is in this very epistle that we have been discussing the various reasons that God allows suffering! Then the preceding verse even says, "But even if you should *suffer* …"

So I would contend that we should first interpret this verse in the context of a person in the midst of suffering. And this is Peter providing us God's instruction for what to do when we are suffering. The last phrase of verse 14 says not to fear like other people do. Rather, "in your heart set apart Christ as Lord." Or, as we discussed above, remember that Jesus is God and sovereign over this situation and we can trust Him in it. And then "be prepared to give an answer to everyone who asks you to give the reason for the hope that you have."

There are a couple of things that we should note. First, this verse is saying that we should expect people to *ask* us about something they are observing in us. And the verse says they will be asking about the "hope that you have." Because this verse is in the context of suffering, I understand this to mean that when people see us enduring suffering with hope and joy, this will grab their attention. They are going to ask something like, "How can you have such peace and hope through something like this?"

This verse is instructing us to "always be ready" to answer that question and give the reason for our hope. And that reason is found in chapter 1 and verses 3 and 4 of this epistle:

> Praise be to the God and Father of our Lord Jesus Christ! In his great mercy he has given us new birth into a living *hope* through the resurrection of Jesus Christ from the dead, and into an inheritance that can never perish, spoil or fade—kept in heaven for you. (emphasis mine)

Thus, as we let our trials shape and form and prune our character, the Lord may be orchestrating an opportunity for us to share the Gospel with someone. Our pain may be bringing about a meeting with someone we otherwise would not have met, or may be creating a situation that brings up the topic of faith with someone we know in such a way that the good news may be heard. The other way we can reach people and "reveal Christ" through a trial of pain or suffering is that the Lord may be preparing us to be a source of sympathy and comfort to a person who is going through their own time of difficulty.[199] Second Corinthians describes it like this:

---

[199] As noted before, there is some degree of overlap between the principles described in this book. In chapter 5, we discussed being sanctified and matured in a way that would allow us to sympathize with others and be a comfort to them under the second principle. This idea of being sanctified in a way to be able to sympathize with and comfort people and actually living it out bridges the gap between principles two and three where the third principle (to "reveal Christ") is being put into practice. I have chosen to discuss this

> Praise be to the God and Father of our Lord Jesus
> Christ, the Father of compassion and the God of
> all comfort, who comforts us in all our troubles, so
> that we can comfort those in any trouble with the
> comfort we ourselves have received from God. For
> just as the sufferings of Christ flow over into our
> lives, so also through Christ our comfort overflows.
> If we are distressed, it is for your comfort and
> salvation; if we are comforted, it is for your comfort,
> which produces in you patient endurance of the
> same sufferings we suffer. And our hope for you is
> firm, because we know that just as you share in our
> sufferings, so also you share in our comfort (1:3–7).

As we receive comfort from God, this enables us to extend that
comfort to others. "Through Christ our comfort overflows!" And
when we have experienced great pain, this has a way of softening
our hearts and giving us a firsthand knowledge of the emotions and
difficulties of trials that enables us to sympathize with others and
even be able to anticipate what may be helpful, encouraging, and
comforting.

I imagine each of us could think of an example of either of
these things playing out. Things that cause pain and suffering can
often lead to a hospital stay which brings people into our lives that
we otherwise would have never met. Could this be an opportunity
to reach someone and share the love of Christ? Or, how many times
have we heard of people who, because of the help they received
during a period of pain and suffering, chose a career or start a
ministry to be able to help people in a similar manner?

At this point let me reiterate principle number three. God may
be bringing you through this time of suffering so that you may

---

aspect of encouraging others under the third principle in this chapter as living
this out, seems to me, to be more in line with sharing the truth of the Gospel
(i.e., principle #3).

be able to reach others for Him. This may happen through an opportunity to share the Gospel where you reveal the *person* of Jesus Christ. Or, this may happen through being a source of comfort and encouragement to someone where you reveal the *compassion* of Jesus Christ.

In light of this, we ought to encourage one another to look for such opportunities—even in the midst of great pain, suffering, and sorrow. Bringing someone to a knowledge of the truth, or providing comfort and encouragement in a time of need, is something worth rejoicing over and may be the way the Lord "turns your sorrow into joy" (John 16:20).

So maybe, just maybe, the Lord is bringing you through whatever trial you are going through and asking you to endure this pain so that He may grow your character and bring you to a place that you can reach someone for Him in a way that otherwise would not be possible. Is that not a reason to encourage us to persevere through our trials and to trust God with the purposes He may have for it?

I hope that we can all see how these truths can strengthen us and help us to see that we can endure suffering, we are called to endure suffering, and we encourage one another through suffering because we have a real hope that is in us—a hope that is worth telling people about (see 1 Peter 3:15). And we will cover that in the next chapter.

8

The Pastoral Problem—Hoping through Pain

"Sorry to interrupt, but are you able to come and speak with him?"
One of my colleagues came and got my attention while I was in a
procedure review meeting. I had been working with an athlete for
several weeks as he was recovering from an anterior cruciate ligament
reconstruction, and he was being seen in the clinic that morning.

"He has several questions that I think you should be the one to
answer," she continued.

"OK, sure. I will be there in a few minutes," I said. I waited for
a reasonable break in discussion in the meeting and then stepped
out to go and talk with him.

"Hey! Good morning," I said. "I hear you have a few questions.
Is everything going all right?"

"Uh, yeah, I guess so. But I just feel like … like I'm behind. I
was thinking I would be way further along than I am. Am I still
on track? And I didn't think that I would still be having pain with
some activities. It's been almost six months now, and it still hurts to
run. The surgeon said that I should be pretty much back to normal
by six months, and I don't feel anywhere near ready to get back on
the field. I'm starting to get nervous that I won't be ready for the

upcoming season. Do you think something is wrong?" he asked with legitimate concern in his voice.

"Ah, yes. I see. Well, first of all, these are good questions to ask. The road of rehabilitation can be a really long one, and it's easy to feel frustrated and discouraged along the way. So I'm happy you brought this up," I started my response, wanting to affirm his concerns to make sure he felt comfortable raising any others in the future.

"Let me answer your last question first. I don't think anything is wrong. I know your surgeon said six months of recovery, and that is very true when it comes to much of the healing that is going on from the surgery. But restoring strength and the level of performance that you are trying to achieve will probably be closer to a year. Also, you are showing consistent improvement in multiple areas, you are not having any changes in swelling, there is no pain at rest, the ligament is clearly intact when we test it, and you are not having any shifting or giving way in your knee. So everything that we see clinically is telling us the ligament is solid. Next, we are trying to walk a delicate line of moving you along consistently into more vigorous activities while respecting the fact that the knee is still building up its strength. It is not uncommon to develop soreness and discomfort—even pain—as the repair is adapting to new levels of activity. This is not an indication of something being wrong but that the tissue is responding to what we are doing. How quickly we are able to move forward really varies from person to person, and we need to listen to the symptoms that you are having to help guide us in that. Yes, many people are running consistently at this point following a surgery like this, but we have been guiding our progression based on *your* response. So we have been going a little slower at this phase. That being said, I am very confident that given your history—the consistency with which you trained before, the fact that you are overall very healthy, and that you have been steadily moving forward now—once we start working on agility exercises and get you back on the field, you will move through those phases very quickly. So all of that to say I understand how this can feel very frustrating because six months away from the things that you enjoy doing can feel like an eternity, but I don't want you to be discouraged. I do not have any concerns, and the things that you are describing are part of the rehabilitation process."

"OK, good," he said with an audible sigh of relief. "That makes me feel a lot better. I was so worried that something was off and that I wouldn't be able to play once the team starts practicing again."

"I'm glad to hear you feel encouraged. Sometimes just knowing that this is normal is helpful, right?" I replied.

"Yeah, for sure. But do you think I will be ready to go for the season?" he asked with a tone that still had some slight anxiety in it.

"We still have five months to get you ready. In my opinion, there is no reason to give up that hope," I said with a sincerity that understands that if the light at the end of the tunnel is extinguished,[200] a person will quickly find themselves in the dark and have reason to despair.

Like this athlete, often what drives us to persevere through hard times is looking toward the final outcome. We can endure a lot when we know that it is working toward something we truly desire. And it is that "not having but wanting" that drives us forward. But

---

[200] In the medical literature, the characteristic of perseverance is usually referred to as "resilience," and there is quite a physiological process that is involved with this that affects brain neurobiology, the immune system, the digestive system, and even the exchange mechanisms of the central nervous system (see Flurin Cathomas, et al., "Neurobiology of Resilience: Interface Between Mind and Body," *Biological Psychiatry* 86, no. 6 (September 2019), 410–420, https://doi.org/10.1016/j.biopsych.2019.04.011). Although this is certainly amazing, my intention here is not to review the physiological mechanisms of resilience. My aim is to describe why all people, no matter their circumstances, can have reason for hope, which gives rise to perseverance (a.k.a. resilience).

if we continually find ourselves in the state of not having, we can quickly become discouraged. So it is really important that we set our expectations correctly and understand what it is that we know we can hope for, because having hope is a really powerful thing to help carry you—or anyone else—through pain, suffering, and trials. And I am not talking about hope in the way modern-day culture often thinks of it. We often hear people saying things like "I hope the weather holds out for our trip," or "I hope I don't get sick," or even "I hope the Lord heals me." This is more aptly expressed as "I wish" or "I desire" these things. The type of hope that I am talking about is the way scripture uses the term *hope*. The kind of hope that is grounded on faith in God as defined for us in the book of Hebrews:

> Now faith is the assurance of things hoped for, the conviction of things not seen. (11:1 NASB)

We see that hope and faith are closely connected, and hope has a future element to it. It is the expression of looking forward to something that is not yet, but with confidence that it will be received. This is the way the apostle Paul describes hope for us in Romans 8:

> But hope that is seen is no hope at all. Who hopes for what he already has? But if we hope for what we do not yet have, we wait for it patiently. (v. 24–25)

Here it becomes important to understand what it is that we can hope for. If God tells us we have reason for hope, we should also listen to what it is that we are hoping for. And at the risk of disappointing many, the things that the Lord tells us we can have confident assurance will come to pass are not comforts on this earth. God does not say that we can hope for riches in this life. He does not say that we can hope for perfect health or even physical healing in this world. He does not tell us to expect a stress-free or carefree life or that we will be spared from all difficulties, troubles, or pain. No. That is not what we are hoping for. Although we certainly desire those things.

The hope we are told to have goes beyond this world and gazes into eternity "looking forward to the city with foundations, whose architect and builder is God" (Hebrews 11:10) and "longing for a better country—a heavenly one" (Hebrews 11:16). Through the remainder of this chapter and to wrap up this book, I want to help us understand a few things about hope the way it is described for us in the Bible. First, there is substance to our hope. We are trusting in and expecting something actual—something real. Then there is reason for our hope. God has given us evidence that demonstrates that we can trust Him to bring into reality that which He promises to do. And He works to assure us of our hope by testing and refining our faith.

What's more is that this hope is freely given as a gift from God. You cannot merit it. You cannot achieve it. You don't need special access to it through a priest or guru. There is no necessary ritual or formula. So, no matter your circumstances, no matter your pain or difficulties, you need only faith in the Lord Jesus Christ, and this hope is yours.

And it is so important that we understand the nature of this hope, because if we misalign our expectations, rather than bolstering us to persevere (like the athlete concerned about his progress after surgery), this will discourage us and potentially lead us into despair. So it is crucial that we understand what this hope is, so that our trials work in us perseverance (Romans 5:3–5) and perseverance may have its perfect work in making us complete (James 1:3–4).

The Substance to Our Hope

Like we discussed in the last chapter, our faith and trust are in God—the creator and sustainer of all things. So, because there is a real being we can trust to bring about His purposes for us, it follows that there is a real God who we place our hope in to bring about what He says is to come. In that sense, the substance we put our hope in is God. That's what we read in 1 Timothy 4:9–10:

> This is a trustworthy saying that deserves full acceptance (and for this we labor and strive), that we have put our hope in the living God, who is the Savior of all men, and especially of those who believe.

I don't want to belabor this point since we have already discussed this. But since this is foundational, it is worth repeating. The source of hope is faith in a God who is real—who is actual. There is substance to what we have our hope in. And what's more is that God does not leave us totally in the dark about what He has purposed for us. He has revealed to us certain aspects of what lies ahead. So there is also substance to what we hope for—we are looking forward to and expecting something actual!

And what is that? Well, there are many things[201] we are told to hope for, like the consummation of our salvation (see 1 Thessalonians 5:8–9) and the restoration of all creation (see Romans 8:21) through the coming of the new heavens and new earth (see Revelation 21:1–2). God has told us that what we experience here is momentary—it is passing (see 2 Corinthians 4:17). And although we do face trials and afflictions here, it will not compare to the eternal weight of glory that awaits us in the new heavens and earth, a place where …

> God Himself will be with [his people] and be their God. He will wipe every tear from their eyes. There

---

[201] My intention here is not to create an exhaustive list of the many, many things we have to hope for that are described in the Bible. I simply want to highlight the fact that we do have things to hope for that are more than we could ask or imagine (Ephesians 3:20)!

will be no more death or mourning or crying or
pain, for the old order of things has passed away.
(Revelation 21:3–4)

And this is an amazing and glorious thing to hope for! So when
we see the wars, the sickness and disease, the crimes that people
commit against one another, the pain and suffering that occurs on
this earth, we rightfully cry out and groan under this bondage to
sin and death (see Romans 8:21–23). But we must not stop there.
We must let the presence of these things drive us to the point that
we fully grasp the reality that there is something wrong in this
world and that there is something wrong in us. The sorrow we face
on this earth is meant to bring us to repentance, which leads us to
salvation (see 2 Corinthians 7:10) and an expectation, a longing, and
an eagerness for the world that is to come (see Romans 8:19).

But we are not only hoping for a restoration of the world around
us—as glorious as that will be. We are also awaiting the redemption
of our bodies (see Romans 8:23). This is perhaps most pertinent to
our primary discussion in this book—physical pain and suffering.

What we understand as the "redemption of our bodies" is
described as part of the final consummation of our salvation in the
aspect of our "glorification."[202] And glorification is understood as
the coming time when we "are finally freed from the very presence
of sin in both body and soul."[203] It's hard to imagine what this will
be like, but in Philippians 3:21, we read,

[The Lord Jesus Christ] … will transform our lowly
bodies so that they will be like his glorious body.

So we have hope—a confident expectation—that our bodies will

---

[202] Please refer to chapter 5 for a discussion of the various aspects and terms
that describe the components of our salvation.

[203] MacArthur and Mayhue, "The Application of Redemption," *Biblical
Doctrine*, 654.

be made like Jesus's resurrection body. It will be imperishable (see 1 Corinthians 15:42). It will be free from pain (see Revelation 21:3). And it will bear the image of the man of heaven (see 1 Corinthians 15:49). Thus, each of our resurrection bodies will be perfect in the sense that it will be restored to its intended design.

At this point, I want to pause and, with as much compassion as I can, explicitly address those people who have been afflicted with chronic conditions or congenital abnormalities. Although most people cannot readily sympathize with your condition, as they have not had to deal with the types of challenges or difficulties that you have had to face, I want to say that there is a very real hope for you. Even if God has asked you to face this world with the ever-present reality of pain, or the constant reminder of the effects of sin through a physical abnormality, He *will* restore your body. He *will* remove your pain. He *will* comfort your sorrows. To some extent, I trust that is happening as you read His Word to you, but to its fullest extent, it will happen in the age to come.

> Therefore we do not lose heart. Though outwardly we are wasting away, yet inwardly we are being renewed day by day. For our light and momentary troubles are achieving for us an eternal glory that far outweighs them all. (2 Corinthians 4:16–17)

The Reason for our Hope

I realize that trusting and believing all of the above, especially when you are in the midst of pain and suffering, is easier said than done. But God, in the richness of His mercy, love, and grace, has given us ample reason to believe all that He has said about the future— namely the hope of new life, new heavens, new earth, and a new body. He has given us evidence to prove His power, to show His love for us, and to demonstrate His victory over death.

First, God has proven His power through the very existence of the world we see around us. We need only open our eyes to the vastness of the universe, the regularity of the orbits of stars and planets, the intricate design of plants and animals, the interdependence of things in nature, and the cycles of the seasons, the tides, the rising of the sun and moon, and the list could go on!

> For since the creation of the world God's invisible qualities—his eternal power and divine nature— have been clearly seen, being understood from what has been made, so that men are without excuse. (Romans 1:20)

God's handiwork is undeniable, albeit some may try to suppress that truth. He has proven His power to us through what He has made.

Then He has shown us clearly how great His love is for us in that He gave His one and only Son for us (John 3:16). It is through that very act of self-sacrifice that we even can comprehend what love is (1 John 3:16). And from here we can reason along with the apostle Paul,

> What, then, shall we say in response to this? If God is for us, who can be against us? He who did not spare his own Son, but gave him up for us all—how will he not also, along with him, graciously give us all things? Who will bring any charge against those whom God has chosen? It is God who justifies. Who is he that condemns? Christ Jesus, who died— more than that, who was raised to life—is at the right hand of God and is also interceding for us. Who shall separate us from the love of Christ? Shall trouble or hardship or persecution or famine or nakedness or danger or sword? As it is written: "For your sake we face death all day long; we are

considered as sheep to be slaughtered." No, in all these things we are more than conquerors through him who loved us. For I am convinced that neither death nor life, neither angels nor demons, neither the present nor the future, nor any powers, neither height nor depth, nor anything else in all creation, will be able to separate us from the love of God that is in Christ Jesus our Lord. (Romans 8:31–39)

Notice the rhetorical question: if God did not spare His own son, will He not also give us all things? The implied answer is yes! Of course, He will also give us all things! And did you notice how what Paul said gave us even more confidence in all of this? That "Christ Jesus ... was raised to life." God has demonstrated His victory over sin and death through the resurrection of Jesus Christ.

In 1 Corinthians, Paul gives a long monologue on the resurrection. He reminds us first that if there is no resurrection, then Christ Himself is not raised (15:13). And if Christ is not raised, we have no reason for our faith—it is "futile, worthless" (15:17). Paul then goes on to say, in effect, that the resurrection gives us hope of the life and world to come by pointing out that if our hope was just for this world, that would be a serious letdown: "If in Christ we have hope in this life only, we are of all people most to be pitied" (15:19).

So it is the resurrection that gives us reason to hope for things that are yet to come—the unseen realities of what God has promised![204] And in closing his discussion of the resurrection, Paul reminds us that the last enemy to be destroyed is death (15:26). But God has

---

[204] For the skeptical reader who is unsure of the fact of the resurrection of Jesus Christ, please see the work of William Lane Craig: "The Historicity of the Empty Tomb of Jesus," *New Testament Studies* 31 (1985): 39–67. "Contemporary Scholarship and the Historical Evidence for the Resurrection of Jesus Christ," *Truth* 1 (1985): 89–95. "The Bodily Resurrection of Jesus," in *Gospel Perspectives I*, ed. R.T. France and D. Wenham (Sheffield, England: JSOT Press, 1980), 47–74.

declared His future victory over that through the resurrection! Paul closes chapter 15 with this:

> When the perishable has been clothed with the imperishable, and the mortal with immortality, then the saying that is written will come true: "Death has been swallowed up in victory." "Where, O death, is your victory? Where, O death, is your sting?" The sting of death is sin, and the power of sin is the law. But thanks be to God! He gives us the victory through our Lord Jesus Christ. Therefore, my dear brothers, stand firm. Let nothing move you. Always give yourselves fully to the work of the Lord, because you know that your labor in the Lord is not in vain. (v. 54–58)

There are two things I want to point out from this passage. First, he says that this ultimate victory is in the future. He says, "then the saying *will come true*" (emphasis mine). The final victory over death is something we are still waiting for, but we are told this will happen at the time of Christ's return with the resurrection of believers. So, again, the reality of Christ's resurrection from the dead gives us reason to hope for the future resurrection and life in the world to come when death will be no more (see Revelation 21:1–4).

Then look at how Paul tells us we should live in light of this truth. He says, "Stand firm. Let nothing move you" and "work for the Lord." He does not say, "Remember this hope, and all things will be hunky-dory, and you will live in ethereal bliss for the rest of your life." No. His imperative to stand firm indicates that there will be things that come against us. We should expect to face things that try to move us away from this hope and that it will take work and labor. But it is persevering through those things that *assures* us of our hope!

The Assurance of Our Hope

Have you ever wondered why we are told to "consider it pure joy when we face trials of many of kinds" (James 1:2)? This verse is often quoted in isolation from the two verses that follow it. Because of this, many people may see this exhortation as counterintuitive. How are we to see the hard things of this life as joyful? The emotions that naturally come when we encounter trials are typically not positive ones, and the Bible even affirms weeping and mourning. So how do we reconcile this? How are we to understand the instruction to be joyful in trials alongside the truth that the presence of grief and sorrow are inevitable? How do we avoid falling into stoicism or a psychological sublimation where we never actually deal with the reality of pain and suffering?

I want to take our time with this concept of how we can have joy in the face of trials because this is a vital part of being able to hope through pain, suffering, and grief. So we are going to examine this passage in James in some detail and also discuss the doctrine of the "perseverance of the saints" or "eternal security" so that anyone reading this who is in the midst of a difficult time may be strengthened to endure, be encouraged to press forward, be assured of their hope, and have joy in light of the reality of that hope.

In doing this, I am going to state clearly what I believe first. Then I will draw that out and reiterate it again. The reason we can have joy when we face trials is because when we are persevering through trials, we have the greatest assurance of the authenticity of our faith that we can have on this earth. To put it another way, the ultimate test of our faith is enduring through trials. So when we see ourselves persevering and our faith in, and love for, God growing, we can be sure of our salvation, which is a tremendous cause for joy!

Now, I imagine some people are furrowing their eyebrows at this statement, so let me draw this out. First of all, we must remember that salvation is by God's grace, which is appropriated to us through faith. Because of that, we do not garner our salvation through saying the right things (although we want to say things that are true) or through doing the right things (although we want to do things that are good and consistent with what we believe). Rather, salvation is appropriated when God works in our hearts such that we believe and trust in the right thing. And that is we must have faith in and trust the only thing that has the power to save us—the person and work of Jesus Christ.

We must remember this:

> There is salvation in no one else, for there is no other name under heaven given among men by which we must be saved. (Acts 4:12 ESV)

And …

> For there is one God, and there is one mediator between God and men, the man Christ Jesus. (1 Timothy 2:5 ESV)

You know you will be saved when you can say this of Jesus and believe that God raised Him from the dead (see Romans 10:9). Because if you believe God raised Him from the dead, you also have reason to believe that Jesus is the Son of God (see Romans 1:4). And if you believe that Jesus is the Son of God, you will also recognize Him as the maker and sustainer of all things (see Colossians 1:16–17) and believe Him when He says, "Whoever believes in him [Jesus] shall not perish but have eternal life" (John 3:16).

Now, it is important to remember that Jesus also said that there will be many people who appear to have faith but do not.[205] And

---

[205] I have in mind here the "Lord, Lord" verses of Matthew 7:21–23, the parable of the wheat and tares in Matthew 13, and the parable of soils in Matthew 13:24–20, 36–43. To keep this chapter from being too long, I have decided not to expound on each of these examples to substantiate the reality of the possibility of "false profession."

Jesus also said that endurance is akin to a final test of faith (see Matthew 24:13). So in that sense, trials may be necessary to prove our faith as genuine, to assure us that we are, in fact, believing the right things. Facing trials will force us to ask ourselves, are we trusting in Jesus because we expect blessing from Him and love the things He gives us?[206] Or are we trusting in Jesus because we love Him for the love that He has shown us? Are we turning to Jesus because we want to do great things? Or are we following Jesus because He is great and He may ask us to glorify Him through doing great things? It is somewhat alarming to understand how deceptive our hearts can be in these things, and that is why trials must come. They must come to work perseverance so that perseverance can finish its perfect work (James 1:4) and our faith may be refined, as by fire, and proved genuine (1 Peter 1:7).

This brings us to our passage in James. So why are we to "consider it pure joy when we face various trials"? If we continue to read the rest of the passage, James actually answers this question for us. He continues in verses 3–4,

> Because you know that the testing of your faith develops perseverance. Perseverance must finish its work so that you may be mature and complete, not lacking anything.

James then gives his readers some practical instructions during these trials and then reiterates this truth in verse 12:

> Blessed is the man who perseveres under trial, because when he has stood the test, he will receive the crown of life that God has promised to those who love him.

---

[206] Remember principle one from chapter 5.

OK, so what is all this saying? What are we to take away from this and why is it cause for joy? And how does it assure us of the hope we have in Jesus? Let's break this down starting with the phrase "when you face trials of many kinds."

So this is an assertion that we *will* face trials—"*when* you face trials." We are to expect them. Jesus tells His disciples that "in this world you *will* have trouble" (John 16:33; emphasis mine). Paul tells Timothy, "Indeed, all who desire to live a godly life in Christ Jesus *will* be persecuted" (1 Timothy 3:12 ESV; emphasis mine). And Peter tells us, "Beloved, *do not be surprised* at the fiery trial *when* it comes upon you to test you, as though something strange were happening to you" (1 Peter 4:12 ESV). Trials and testing are part and parcel with the Christian walk because we live in a fallen world and are in a fallen condition and the days are evil (see Ephesians 5:15–16).

And this is super important to remember. If we are expecting that the Christian life is going to be blessed with perfect health and wealth and be carefree and stress-free, we have set our expectations wrong. God certainly promises blessing but not necessarily in those ways in this life. Let's return to our introductory story for an example of why it's important to have accurate expectations. When this young man was experiencing something inconsistent with what he expected, he began to be concerned that something was wrong. He was concerned that he was falling behind. Perhaps the surgery was failing, or he was not healing appropriately. In a similar way, if we expect that our Christian walk is supposed to be filled with material blessing or healing from all ailments if we have enough faith, this creates an expectation that discourages us when we encounter trials. By default, this perspective teaches you to question your faith when trials come, whereas the Bible says that trials will come, and when they do, if you truly believe, it will strengthen your faith—it will "finish its work so that you may be mature and complete."

Then, not only are we to expect trials, but they can be "of many kinds." These trials may come through sickness, injury, financial difficulty, conflict in relationship, loss of work, natural disaster leading to loss of material things, you name it. All of those things that bring difficulties into our lives can serve this purpose, and we can expect to encounter trials of many kinds and in varying degrees. In the context of this book, we have mostly been discussing trials in the form of physical pain (i.e., injury or illness). And I want to focus on this for a moment in light of our discussion of appropriate expectations regarding faith, trials, and some of the teaching that exists surrounding faith healing. My concern with any teaching that says that it is always God's will to heal you is that it leads to a wrongful expectation of the Christian walk.[207] This type of teaching places the assurance of your faith on the *healing*, which is actually contrary to the Bible, because the Bible tells us to be assured by the *persevering* (whether or not physical healing comes in this life).[208]

Moving on to verses 3 and 4, we see Paul answer our initial question, "How can we be joyful even during trials?" He says here,

> Because you know the testing of your faith develops
> perseverance. Perseverance must finish its work so
> that you may be mature and complete, not lacking
> anything.

Notice that it is not because of the trial that we are to have joy. We are not to try to cultivate some kind of positive emotional response to difficult things where we say, "Yay, I'm sick!" or "I am *so* happy that I am in pain right now." We are not being instructed

---

[207] To be clear, I am referring to physical healing in this world. Certainly, it is God's will to heal all believers in an ultimate sense when He returns to establish His kingdom (see Revelation 21:1–4). However, the emphasis by some teachers is on physical healing now. That is the specific teaching that I am addressing here.

[208] I am not saying that miraculous healings do not happen or cannot happen. I am saying, however, that we should not demand miraculous healings always or for all believers. The apostle Paul is a clear case in point: God did not heal Paul's "thorn in the flesh" (see 2 Corinthians 12).

to live in denial here. We can still recognize the reality of pain and suffering with sorrow and grief and have joy and hope because our joy is found in our salvation, not in our circumstances. And what Paul is saying here in verse 2 is that our joy is to be over what the trial is doing in us and assuring us of; it is testing us and maturing us.

Trials will indicate to us the "soil" of our heart (see Matthew 13:1–23). When cares and troubles come, is the seed of faith "choked out" by these "weeds and thistles"? Or does our faith flourish and grow? And if it grows, we can be assured that our faith has taken root in a healthy soil that is nourished by Christ. In Luke's accounting of this parable, Jesus continues with the parable of the lamp, stating that the light of a lampstand is meant to reveal (Luke 8:16–18). Thus, I suggest that our responses to trials and the way we respond to the message of Christ during the trials we face on earth are to be an indicator to us. Like the light from a lampstand reveals what is otherwise in the dark, trials show us the kind of "soil" that is making up of our hearts.

And a heart of fertile soil cultivates the sort of faith that remembers that we have been given "the Holy Spirit, who is a deposit guaranteeing our inheritance" (Ephesians 1:13–14). This faith understands that we belong to Christ, who is the Good Shepherd, and we are "his sheep" to whom He gives eternal life, and no one will snatch us out of His hand (John 10:27–29). This faith believes that "He who began a good work in you will carry it on to completion until the day of Christ Jesus" (Philippians 1:6).

These passages help us to formulate the doctrine known as the "perseverance of the saints" or "eternal security." What this teaches is that if you have been saved by God, you cannot lose your salvation—you will *persevere*, and your salvation is *eternally secure*. This doctrine puts the emphasis of salvation on God saving us, rather than us clinging to God. In other words, we are saved because of God's work, not our decision to invite God into our life or our ability to cling to God during hard times. And this should be very reassuring to all of us. Because what this teaches is that you need not be worried if you slip, or fall, or make a mistake, or sin from time to time.[209] Living perfectly or having some arbitrary amount of faith is not what saves you. But your faith in the right person will. And we know that person, Jesus Christ, will pick you up, carry you, and forgive you in times of difficulty, trials, and failures. And this should affirm to you that you have received God's grace.

And we can hold firmly to our faith because ...

> We do not have a high priest who is unable to sympathize with our weaknesses, but we have one who has been tempted in every way, just as we are—yet was without sin. Let us then approach the throne of grace with confidence, so that we may receive mercy and find grace to help us in our time of need. (Hebrews 4:15–16)

Jesus is gentle and lowly and invites us to come to Him when we are weary and burdened (see Matthew 11:28–30), and He will give us the assurance of the "Sabbath-rest that remains for God's people" (Hebrews 4:9). I am confident that no matter what you are facing while reading this, if you turn to Christ, believing *that* He is and *who* He is, you will receive the mercy and grace you need.

Now, the other side of understanding the doctrine of the perseverance of the saints is that if a person, in their trials, begins to turn from God, deny His goodness, or ultimately deny that Jesus

---

[209] Please don't take this to mean that I am rationalizing the license to continue to sin. By no means! I am saying that because sin remains in our nature, we will at times stumble into sin. But because of God's Spirit in us, when we are made aware of this, we will repent, and our character will grow—we will be transformed more and more into the likeness of Christ. My point here is that the presence of sin in our lives is not an indicator that we have not been saved; quite the contrary. If you are recognizing more and more sin in your life, are mourning over that sin, and being driven to repentance more often, you actually should be assured of God's saving work in you!

is the Christ, this is an indicator that he was never actually saved to begin with (see 1 John 2:18–22). These people may have confessed Christ as Savior with their mouth but not actually believed in their hearts. These people may have even done great and amazing things while professing faith (see Matthew 7:21–23). But if they do not endure and persevere in their faith in Jesus, they have failed the test (see 2 Corinthians 13:5) because Jesus says that those "who *endure* to the end shall be saved" (Matthew 24:13).

So when we see ourselves being drawn to God and trusting Him more, which allows us to persevere through our trials, we know that our heart is being revealed to us and assures us that we are passing the test of faith. And when we have "stood the test," we know that we "will receive the crown of life that God has promised to those who love him" (James 1:12). So it is that our perseverance through trials assures us of the hope we have, which is a tremendous cause for joy!

> Consider it pure joy, my brothers, whenever you
> face trials of many kinds.

Conclusion

A Purported Problem

"So how much would you like me to modify the protocol for him?"
I had just hunted down one of the surgeons I work with, as I had
just started seeing one of his patients in the clinic. From reading
the operative note, I saw that the procedure had been modified.
And the patient had been instructed to remain non-weight bearing
significantly longer than what I was used to.

"A *lot!*" came the quick reply. "I want you to progress his activity
very slowly. Here, let me pull up some photos from the surgery and
walk you through what I did."

This patient had sustained a rupture of his quadriceps tendon
and delayed seeking care for several days. Then, when he did go in
to have it looked at, he had ignored his symptoms to such an extent
that he was walking and moving around well enough that the initial
provider assumed it was only a minor injury. Because of this, he
was not urgently referred for a surgical consult. By the time he was
evaluated by the surgeon, the tendon had retracted to such an extent
that a modified procedure was necessary to repair the tendon.

"OK, I thought we were going to have to go slow!" I replied with
much greater appreciation for the healing process this young man
was undergoing. "But that's part of the reason I wanted to catch

up with you. He is already walking around without his brace or crutches, despite my reminders not to."

"This guy is something else!" the surgeon said with an exasperated tone. "Hasn't he had several revision surgeries to his other knee and shoulder before this too?" he asked, with some degree of amazement in his voice.

"Yes." I let out a sigh of acknowledgment. "I have worked with him after three of those surgeries. He does not seem to recognize any limits. And, unfortunately, he doesn't seem to experience much pain during his recovery to help slow him down. Then when he does feel pain, he will often just respond by saying, 'Well, no pain, no gain, right?' I will do my best to tell him again that he needs time to heal and that we want to listen to the signals his body is giving him through his pain."

One of the primary reasons for pain, physiologically, is to warn us of potential damage to our bodies. It is therefore so important that we understand why we are experiencing pain to know how to address it. Physical pain is often produced by our bodies to slow us down, reduce our activity, and force upon us the necessary rest for healing.[210] And if we ignore that, we risk future and further injury. This unfortunately played out on several occasions for this young man.

It is not often that we think of pain as a good thing, but in the face of danger, it is a powerful stimulus that gets our attention. Dr. Paul Brand, in writing his memoirs on his career treating leprosy,

---

[210] As a reminder, sometimes the way our body processes sensations leads to the production of pain that is not indicative of any actual damage (see chapter 7). So there will be times that it is good and necessary to work through pain or where we do not yield to this signal like we would in this situation. It is a very important part of my job to discern the difference between these situations.

titled his book *The Gift of Pain.*[211] In this work, he describes the disease as one that essentially deadens the nerves and reduces or eliminates the patient's ability to feel pain—usually in patients' hands, feet, and face. Because of this, he discovered that the physical maladies that patients would experience—things like sores, open wounds, loss of fingers and toes—were not the direct results of the disease. Rather, they would occur from patients not noticing they had cut themselves, or scratched away at a scab to cause further damage, or were touching a hot stove. Their inability to feel pain made it such that they were unable to perceive the warning signals all of us usually experience, and the result was tremendous harm.[212]

So why do *we* hurt? Because there is a danger—a threat—in this world that we need to be made aware of. This world is fallen and sinful and must be redeemed—just like us. This world is not our final home, and the constant reminder of death and disaster keeps us looking forward, setting our eyes on heaven, and waiting with an eager expectation for the world to come. The pain we experience is warning us of the dangers in this world, prompting us to keep our hope and expectation on things above.

Why do *you* hurt? Because God is proving your faith, leading you to repentance, and developing your character so that you may be a witness, comfort, and source of encouragement to those around you.

Why does God let this continue? Because "the Lord is not slow to fulfill his promise as some count slowness, but is patient toward you, not wishing that any should perish, but that all should

---

[211] Dr. Paul Brand and Philip Yancey, *The Gift of Pain: Why we hurt & what we can do about it* (Grand Rapids, MI: Zondervan, 1997).

[212] It is no wonder that the Bible uses leprosy as a picture of sin. If one continues in a state of sin, it is possible to become less sensitive to its effects (see Ephesians 4:19) and can even 'sear our consciences' (cf. 1 Timothy 4:2). This communicates the idea of being unable to feel the effects of sin morally. And the result of an unawareness of the warning signs of pain that result from sin is further harm!

reach repentance" (2 Peter 3:9). By allowing pain to continue, He is drawing more people to Him and bringing salvation to more.

Does the reality of pain present a problem that we should address? Yes.

What should we do about the pain and suffering we see? "[We] ought to live holy and godly lives as [we] look forward to the day of God and speed its coming" (2 Peter 3:11–12). Lives characterized by this will comfort people in pain, stand with and encourage one another through suffering, lead people to repentance when sinful behavior is evident, and remind people of the God who is sovereign over it all and will bring about the end of pain and suffering in the world to come.

Does the reality of pain present an insurmountable problem to the teachings of Christianity? No.

I trust that what has been presented in this book has helped you to see that although the reality of evil, pain, and suffering is uncomfortable and brings with it much sadness and grief, it does not undercut the teachings of Christianity, nor is it inconsistent with the reality of a good and loving God. In fact, the experience of pain and suffering helps us to understand the love of God our Father and actually sets apart the Christian response from all other religious and philosophical responses. How is that?

When we experience trials of pain and suffering, we have an opportunity to "share in Jesus's suffering" (Philippians 3:10). This should help us to understand the immense pain that Jesus endured for us (see Hebrews 12:2–3). And this is unique to the Christian response. Jesus, the Son of God, God incarnate, has humbled Himself by taking on the form of man (see Philippians 2:6–11) and experienced pain, suffering, and sorrow not only with us but for us. He can sympathize with whatever we face in this life (see Hebrews 4:15) and has taken for us a much greater form of suffering on the cross (see 1 Peter 3:18). Because of this, He can go alongside us as we run the race of faith in this life (see Hebrews 12:1).

And when we grasp the reality of what Jesus has done for us, the only right response to that is love and gratefulness to our Savior. Such a response will grant us peace and encouragement so that we "do not grow weary or lose heart" (Hebrews 12:3).

Rather, it will enable us to …

> Endure hardship as discipline; God is treating you as sons. For what son is not disciplined by his father? If you are not disciplined (and everyone undergoes discipline), then you are illegitimate children and not true sons. Moreover, we have all had human fathers who disciplined us and we respected them for it. How much more should we submit to the Father of our spirits and live! Our fathers disciplined us for a little while as they thought best; but God disciplines us for our good, that we may share in his holiness. No discipline seems pleasant at the time, but painful. Later on, however, it produces a harvest of righteousness and peace for those who have been trained by it. Therefore, strengthen your feeble arms and weak knees. (Hebrews 12:7–12)

So, to all who are reading this now, as we seek to persevere through the pain and suffering in this world, I can think of no better way to encourage and strengthen you than to point you to Jesus Christ and close with God's Word to us:

> Let us fix our eyes on Jesus, the author and perfecter of our faith, who for the joy set before him endured the cross, scorning its shame, and sat down at the right hand of the throne of God. Consider Him who endured such opposition from sinful men, so that you will not grow weary and lose heart. (Hebrews 12:2–3)

And as we persevere through the trials the Lord asks us to face, may we grow in fellowship with Him as we understand the suffering He endured for us all the more, and may our eagerness for His coming increase. And, as we await His return may we remember His word to us:

In this world you will have trouble. But take heart!
I have overcome the world. (John 16:33)

Amen, and come, Lord Jesus!